Exercises *Second Edition*
in Helping Skills

A Training Manual to Accompany The Skilled Helper

Exercises *Second Edition*
in Helping Skills

A Training Manual to Accompany The Skilled Helper

Gerard Egan

Loyola University of Chicago

Brooks/Cole Publishing Company
Monterey, California

ISBN: 0-8185-0480-3

Printed in the United States of America

10 9 8 7 6 5 4 3 2 1

Contents

Exercises *Second Edition*
in Helping Skills

A Training Manual to Accompany The Skilled Helper

INTRODUCTION

The exercises in this manual are meant to accompany the revised edition of The Skilled Helper by Gerard Egan (Brooks/Cole Publishing Company, Monterey, California, 1981) and Systematic Helping by Gerard Egan (Brooks/Cole Publishing Company, forthcoming). These exercises serve a number of purposes:

(1) They can help you develop a behavioral rather than merely a cognitive grasp of the principles, skills, and methods that turn helping models into useful tools.

(2) They can be used by you to help you explore your own strengths and weaknesses as a helper. That is, they provide a way of having you apply the helping model to yourself first before trying it out on others. As such, they can help you confirm your strengths and manage weaknesses that would stand in the way of your becoming an effective helper.

(3) You can help clients use these exercises to explore and manage their own problems in living more effectively. Used in this way, these exercises can promote better client participation in the helping process.

(4) You can help clients use these exercises to learn the skills of problem management themselves. This kind of training-as-treatment can encourage self-responsibility in clients and help make them less dependent on others in managing their lives.

A TRAINING PROGRAM

The following are standard steps in a skills-training program:

(1) Trainees first get a cognitive understanding of a particular skill or counseling method. This can be done by reading and listening to lectures.

(2) Trainees are then given an opportunity to clarify what they have read or heard. This can be done through questioning and discussion.

The objective of Steps 1 and 2 is cognitive clarity.

(3) Then trainers model the skill or method in question. This can be done "live" or through films and videotapes.

(4) Trainees are next asked to use the skill they have read about and seen demonstrated in an initial way. This is to see that they understand the skill enough to begin to practice it.

The objective of Steps 3 and 4 is behavioral clarity.

(5) Trainees are divided up into smaller groups to practice the skill or method in question with one another.

(6) During these practice sessions trainees receive feedback from a trainer and from one another. This feedback serves to confirm what they are doing right and to correct what they are doing wrong. The use of video to provide feedback is most helpful.

(7) Finally, from time to time trainees are asked to stop and reflect on the training process itself. They are given an opportunity to express how they feel about how training is going and how they feel about their own progress. While Steps 1 through 6 deal with the task of the training group, Step 7 deals with maintenance, that is, seeing to the feelings and needs of individual trainees.

The exercises in this manual can be used between Steps 4 and 5 as a way of practicing the skills and methods "in private" before practicing them with your fellow trainees. They provide a behavioral link between the initial introduction to a skill or method that takes place in Steps 1 through 4 and actual practice in a group.

THE EIGHT TASKS OF EFFECTIVE HELPING

For the most part the exercises presented here are grouped around and follow the order of the eight tasks that need to be undertaken in the effective management of problem situations. These tasks are:

1. _Assessment_. This means helping clients find out what's going wrong _and_ what's going right in their lives. Successful assessment helps clients identify both problems and resources. Assessment helps clients see any given problem in a wider _context_. Assessment goes on _throughout_ the helping process.

2. _Focusing and initial problem exploration_. This means helping clients _identify_ the particular concern or concerns they want to deal with and beginning the exploration and clarification process.

3. _New perspectives:_ This means helping clients see themselves, their concerns, and the context of their concerns more objectively, that is, in such a way as to begin to see what they would like to do about them.

Steps 1, 2, and 3, therefore, deal with _problem identification and clarification_.

4. _Goal setting_. This means helping clients set problem-managing goals. A goal is nothing else but _what_ a client wants to _accomplish_ in order to manage a problem situation or some part of it more effectively.
A goal refers to _what_ a client would like to do about a problem situation. The next two steps taken together constitute _program development_. Program development deals with _how_ clients might go about accomplishing their goals.

5. _Program possibilities_. This refers to helping clients see the many different ways that any given goal can be accomplished. It also refers to helping clients identify the resources available for accomplishing goals.

6. _Program choice_. This refers to helping clients choose the kind of program that _best fits_ their style, resources, and environment.

7. _Program implementation_. This refers to helping clients implement the programs they have chosen and helping them overcome the obstacles they encounter as they do so.

8. _Evaluation_. This refers to helping clients monitor their participation in programs, their accomplishment of goals, and their management of problem situations.

YOUR ROLE AS TRAINEE: DEALING WITH REAL CONCERNS

One way of learning these eight tasks is to apply them to yourself and your own problems and concerns first. This means placing yourself in the role of a client. There are two ways of doing this. You can pretend to be a client or you can really become a client. Since this distinction is important, let us look at it more carefully.

Role-playing versus dealing with real concerns. As a trainee, you are going to be asked to act both as a helper and as a client in practice sessions. In the written exercises in this manual, you are asked at one time or another to play each of these roles. There are two ways of playing the role of the client:

1. you can role-play, that is pretend to have certain problems, or
2. you can discuss your own real problems and concerns.

Role-playing, although not easy, is still less personally demanding than discussing your own real life concerns in practice sessions. However, although some role-playing might be useful at the beginning of the training process (since it is less threatening and allows you to ease yourself into the role of client), I suggest that you eventually use the training process to look at some of the real problems or concerns in your own life, especially problems or characteristics of interpersonal style that might interfere with your effectiveness as a helper. For instance, if you tend to be an impatient person--one who places unreasonable demands on others--you will have to examine and change this behavior if you want to become an effective helper. Or if you are very nonassertive, this could keep you from helping clients make reasonable demands on themselves.

Learning what it means to be a client. Another reason for using real problems or concerns when you take the role of the client is that it gives you some experience of being a client. Then when you face real clients, you can appreciate some of the misgivings they might have in talking about the intimate details of their lives to a relative stranger. Other things being equal, I would personally prefer going to a helper who has had some experience in being a client.

The safe and productive training group. Dealing with personal concerns in the training sessions will be both safe and productive if you have a competent trainer who provides adequate supervision for this process, if the training group becomes a learning community which provides both support and reasonable challenge for its members, and if you are willing to discuss personal concerns. Self-disclosure will be counterproductive if you let others extort it from you or if you attempt to extort it from others. Your self-disclosure should always remain appropriate to the goals of the training group. "Secret-dropping" and dramatic self-disclosure are not functional approaches to taking the role of client.

Preparing for self-disclosure. If you are to talk about yourself during the practice sessions, you should take some care in choosing what you are going to reveal about yourself. Making some preparation for what you are going to say can prevent you from revealing things about yourself that you would rather not. Here is a limited sample of the kinds of problems, issues, and concerns that trainees have dealt with during the training process.

* I'm shy. My shyness takes the form of being afraid to meet strangers and being afraid to reveal myself to others.
* I'm a fairly compliant person. Others can push me around and get away with it.
* I get angry fairly easily and let my anger spill out on others in irresponsible ways. I think my anger is often linked to my not getting my own way.
* I'm a lazy person. I find it especially difficult to expend the kind of energy necessary to listen to and get involved with others.
* I'm somewhat fearful of persons of the opposite sex. This is especially true if I think they are putting some kind of demand on me for closeness. I get nervous and try to get away.
* I'm a rather insensitive person, or so I have been told. I'm a kind of bull-in-the-china-shop type. Not much tact.
* I'm overly controlled. I don't let my emotions show very much. Sometimes I don't even want to know what I am feeling myself.
* I like to control others, but I like to do so in subtle ways. I want to stay in charge of interpersonal relationships at all times.
* I have a strong need to be liked by others. I seldom do anything that might offend others or that others would not approve of. I want to be accepted.
* I have few positive feelings about myself. I put myself down in a variety of ways. I get depressed a lot.
* I never stop to examine my values. I think I hold some conflicting values. I'm not even sure why I'm interested in becoming a helper.
* I feel almost compelled to help others. It's part of my religious background. It's as if I didn't even have a choice.
* I'm sensitive, easily hurt. I think I send out messages to others that say "be careful of me."
* I'm overly dependent on others. My self-image depends too much on what others think of me.
* A number of people see me as a "difficult" person. I'm highly individualistic. I'm ready to fight if anyone imposes on my freedom.
* I'm anxious a lot of the time. I'm not even sure why. My palms sweat a lot in interpersonal situations.
* I see myself as a rather colorless, uninteresting person. I'm bored with myself at times and I assume that others are bored with me.
* I'm somewhat irresponsible. I take too many risks, especially risks that involve others. I'm very impulsive. That's probably a nice way of saying that I lack self-control.
* I'm very stubborn. I have fairly strong opinions. I argue a lot and try to get others to see things my way. I argue about very little things.
* I don't examine myself or my behavior very much. I'm usually content with the way things are. I don't expect too much of myself or of others.
* I can be sneaky in my relationships with others. I seduce people in different ways--not necessarily sexual--by my "charm." I get them to do what I want.
* I like the good life. I'm pretty materialistic and I like my own comfort. I don't often go out of my way to meet the needs of others.
* I'm somewhat lonely. I don't think others like me, if they think about me at all. I spend time feeling sorry for myself.
* I'm awkward in social situations. I don't do the right thing at the right time. I don't know what others are feeling when I'm with them and I guess I seem callous.

* Others see me as "out of it" a great deal of the time. I guess I am fairly naive. Others seem to have deeper or more interesting experiences than I do. I think I've grown up too sheltered.
* I'm stingy with both money and time. I don't want to share what I have with others. I'm pretty selfish.
* I'm somewhat of a coward. I sometimes find it hard to stand up for my convictions even when I meet light opposition. It's easy to get me to retreat.
* I hate conflict. I'm more or less a peace-at-any-price person. I run when things get heated up.
* I don't like it when others tell me I'm doing something wrong. I usually feel attacked and I attack back.

This list is not exhaustive, but you can use it to stimulate your thinking about yourself and the kinds of dissatisfactions, problems, or concerns you may have about yourself, especially concerns that might relate to your effectiveness as a helper. The exercises that follow will help you assess your satisfactions and dissatisfactions with yourself and your behavior. You can then choose the issues that you would like to explore during the training sessions.

Some Cautions

First, it is important to note that the exercises suggested in this manual are neither exhaustive nor cast in stone. They are useful to the degree that they help you acquire and improve the kinds of skills that will make you an effective helper. Other exercises can be added and the ones outlined here can be modified in order to achieve this goal more effectively.

Second, these exercises have been written as an adjunct to the text. They often presuppose information in the text that is not repeated in the exercises.

Third, there may not be time to do all these exercises. What can be done depends on the length of the training program in which you are involved. However, a fairly wide sampling of these exercises can help you develop a behavioral feeling for the kinds of skills involved in competent helping.

Fourth, this helping model is developmental. Just as the quality of work in Stage III depends on what has been done in Stages I and II, so the exercises later in the manual depend on the competencies that earlier exercises help you to learn.

Fifth, these exercises achieve their full effect only if you share them with the members of your training group and receive feedback. Your instructor will set up the kind of structure to help you do this. Since time limitations are always an issue, learning how to give brief, concise, behavioral feedback in a human way is most important.

Finally, many of the exercises, especially the exercises from goal setting on, depend on your willingness to work on real problems and concerns. Therefore, it is essential to identify early in the program issues you would be willing to work on in the training group.

TASK 1: ASSESSMENT AND PROBLEM IDENTIFICATION

If you are going to help your clients manage their lives more
effectively, you must be able to help them discover both what is going
wrong <u>and</u> what is going <u>right</u> in their lives. This is called <u>assessment</u>
and <u>problem identification</u>. You have two tasks right from the beginning
of the helping process: (1) to develop the kind of <u>relationship</u> with
your clients that enables them to cooperate as fully as possible in the
kind of problem-management process outlined in <u>The Skilled Helper</u> and
<u>Systematic Helping</u>, and (2) to help them identify and clarify the problem
situations they are trying to manage.

The exercises in this section are designed to help you identify
problem situations and make some preliminary assessment of your own
strengths and weaknesses. You can use them, first of all, to help
<u>yourself</u> identify the problematic issues of your own life that might
stand in the way of helping others. Careful execution of at least some
of the exercises in this section will give you a list of problems or
concerns that are neither too superficial nor too intimate for the
training group. Once you learn how to identify and clarify your own
problems in living, you can use these exercises to help your clients do
the same, especially when they are having trouble doing so. Once you get
a feeling for these exercises yourself, you will know which ones may help
your clients.

EXERCISE 1: <u>What is going wrong and what is going right in my life</u>

Sometimes a very simple structure can help you and your clients
identify the major dimensions of a problem situation. This exercise asks
you to identify some of the things that are not going as well as you
would like them to go in your life ("what's going wrong") and some of the
things you believe you are handling well ("what's going right"). It is
important right from the beginning to help clients become aware of their
resources and successes as well as their problems and their failures.
Problems can be handled more easily if they are seen in the wider context
of competence and resources.

In this exercise, merely jot down in whatever way they come to you
things that are going right and things that could be going better for
you. In order to stress the positive, see if you can write down at least
two things that are going right for everything you see going wrong. Read
the list in the example on the next page and then do your own. Don't
worry whether the problems or concerns you list are really important.
Jot down whatever comes to your mind. Your own list may include some
items similar to those in the example, but it may be quite different
because it will reflect you and not someone else.

Example

What Is Going Right

I have a lot of friends.

I have a decent job and people like the work I do.
Others can count on me; I'm dependable.
I have a reasonable amount of intelligence.
I have no major financial difficulties; I'm secure.
My wife and I get along fairly well.
I am very healthy.
My belief in God gives me a kind of center in life, a stability.

What Is Going Wrong

I seem to have a very negative attitude toward myself.
I get dependent on others much too easily.
My life seems boring too much of the time.
I am afraid to take risks.

What Is Going Right

_____

_____

_____

_____

_____

_____

_____

_____

_____

_____

_____

_____

_____

What Is Going Wrong

_____

_____

_____

_____

_____

_____

_____

_____

_____

_____

_____

_____

_____

EXERCISE 2: Reviewing the developmental tasks of life and the social
settings in which they take place

In your efforts to manage your own life more effectively and to help
others do the same, it is useful to have a comprehensive model of human
functioning to listen to your own experience and that of others in a
focused way. What you "hear" can be organized in terms of strengths and
resources, on the one hand, and of weaknesses, concerns, and problems, on
the other. Exercises 2, 3, 4, and 5 are based on the People in Systems
model developed by Egan and Cowan (Monterey, Calif.: Brooks/Cole, 1979)
and are designed to help you listen to your own experience in a focused
way in terms of (1) the developmental tasks you face at your current
stage of life, (2) the social settings in which you live out your life,
and (3) the life skills you need to carry out these developmental tasks
and involve yourself in growthful ways in these social settings.

This exercise is a kind of checklist that can be used to take a
comprehensive "radar scan" of important areas of your life with a view to
identifying both resources and concerns. The purpose of the people-in-
systems model is to help you see your own, and eventually your clients',
concerns in as wide a context as possible.

In Exercise 2 you are asked to consider your experience with respect
to ten major developmental tasks of adult life (see Egan and Cowan,
Moving Into Adulthood, Monterey, Calif.: Brooks/Cole, 1980 for a fuller
treatment of these tasks) and the social settings in which these tasks
are carried out. Again, it is most important that you identify strengths
as well as "soft" spots in these developmental areas. Use extra paper as
needed.

1. Competence: What Do I Do Well? Do I see myself as a person who is
capable of getting things done? Do I have the resources needed to
accomplish goals I set for myself? In what areas of life do I excel? In
what areas of life would I want to be more competent than I am?

        Strengths   Weaknesses

_____   _____

_____   _____

_____   _____

2. Autonomy: Can I Make It On My Own? Can I get things done on my
own? Do I avoid being overly dependent or independent? Am I reasonably
interdependent in my work and social life? When I need help, do I find
it easy to ask for it? In what social settings do I find myself most
dependent? counterdependent? independent? interdependent?

        Strengths   Weaknesses

_____   _____

_____   _____

_____   _____

3. <u>Values: What Do I Believe In?</u>   What are my values? Do I allow for reasonable changes in my value system? Do I put my values into practice? Do any of my values I hold conflict with others? In what social settings do I pursue the values that are most important to me?

Strengths   Weaknesses

_____   _____

_____   _____

_____   _____

4. <u>Identity: Who Am I In This World?</u>   Do I have a good sense of who I am and the direction I'm going in life? Do the ways that others see me fit with the ways in which I see myself? Do I have some kind of center that gives meaning to my life? In what social settings do I have my best feelings for who I am? In what social settings do I lose my identity?

Strengths   Weaknesses

_____   _____

_____   _____

_____   _____

_____   _____

5. <u>Intimacy: What Are My Closer Relationships Like?</u>   What kinds of closeness do I have with others? Do I have acquaintances, friends, and intimates? What is my life in my peer group like? Are there other social groups in my life? What is life like in them?

Strengths   Weaknesses

_____   _____

_____   _____

_____   _____

6. <u>Sexuality: Who Am I As a Sexual Person?</u>   To what degree am I satisfied with my sexual identity, my sexual preferences, and my sexual behavior? How do I handle my sexual needs and wants? What social settings influence the ways I act sexually?

Strengths   Weaknesses

_____   _____

_____   _____

_____   _____

_____   _____

7. <u>Love, Marriage, Family: What Are My Deeper Commitments in Inter-personal Living</u>? What is my marriage like? How do I relate to my parents and siblings? How do I feel about the quality of my family life?

Strengths   Weaknesses

_____   _____

_____   _____

_____   _____

8. <u>Career: What Is the Place of Work In My Life</u>? How do I feel about the way I am preparing myself for a career? How do I feel about my present position or career? What do I get out of work? What is my workplace like?

Strengths   Weaknesses

_____   _____

_____   _____

_____   _____

9. <u>Investment in the Wider Community: How Big Is My World</u>? How do I invest myself in the world outside of friends, work, and the family? What is my neighborhood like? Do I have community, civic, political, social involvements or concerns?

Strengths   Weaknesses

_____   _____

_____   _____

_____   _____

10. <u>Leisure: What Do I Do With My Free Time</u>? Do I feel that I have sufficient free time? How do I use my leisure? What do I get out of it? In what social settings do I spend my free time?

Strengths   Weaknesses

_____   _____

_____   _____

_____   _____

_____   _____

In your opinion, which strengths that you have noted will help you be a more effective counselor? In what specific ways?

_____

_____

_____

_____

_____

_____

_____

_____

In your opinion, which weaknesses or problems you have noted might stand in the way of your being an effective helper? In what specific ways?

_____

_____

_____

_____

_____

_____

_____

_____

_____

_____

_____

EXERCISE 3: Conflicts in the network of the social settings of life

(1) Charting the Social Settings of Life. Since you are a member of
a number of different social settings and since each places certain
demands on you, conflicts can arise between two or more settings. In
this exercise you are asked to write your name in the middle of a sheet of
paper. Then, as in the example (Figure 1), draw spokes out to the
various social settings of your life. The person in the example is
Mitch, 45, a principal of an inner-city high school in a large city. He
is married and has two teenage sons neither of whom attends the high
school of which he is principal. He is seeing a counselor because of
exhaustion and bouts of hostility and depression. He has had a complete
physical check-up and there is no evidence of any medical problem.
(2) Reviewing expectations, demands, concerns. Now take each social
setting and write down the expectations people have of you in that
setting, the demands they place on you, the concerns you have, the
dissatisfactions expressed to you. For instance, some of the things Mitch
writes are:

Faculty

* Some faculty members want a personal relationship with me and I have
neither the time nor the desire.
* Some faculty members have retired "in place." I don't know what to do
with them.
* Some of the white faculty members are suspicious of me and distant
just because I'm black.
* One faculty member wrote the district superintendent and said that I
was spreading false stories about her. This is not true.

Family

* My wife says that I'm letting school consume me; she complains
constantly because I don't spend enough time at home.
* My kids accuse me of giving in to the "establishment," whatever that
means.

Parents

* My mother is infirm; my retired father calls me and tells me what a
hard time he's having getting used to retirement.
* My mother tells me not to be spending time with her when I have so
much to do and then she complains to my wife and my father when I don't
show up.

Mitch goes on to list demands, expectations, concerns, and
frustrations that relate to each of the settings he has listed on his
chart.
On a separate sheet of paper, list the demands, expectations, and
concerns related to each of the social settings you have on your chart.
Do not try to solve any of the problems you see cropping up. If some
solution to a problem you have does suggest itself while you are doing
this exercise, jot it down and put it aside.

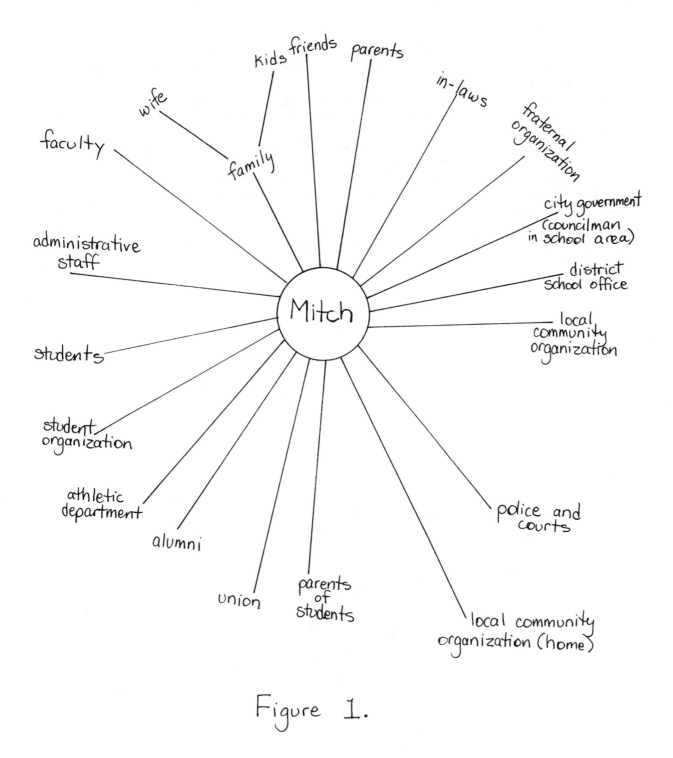

Figure 1.

(3) <u>Identifying conflicts between systems</u>. Once you review the expectations, demands, and concerns associated with each setting, list the conflicts <u>between settings</u> that cause you concern.

Here are some of the conflicts Mitch identifies:
* My wife wants me to spend more time at home and yet she criticizes me for not spending more time with my parents.
* The students, both individually and through their organizations, keep asking me to be more liberal while their parents are asking me to tighten things up.
* My administrative staff thinks that I'm taking sides against them in a dispute with the athletic department.
* My friends say that I spend so much time at work involving myself in crisis management that I have no time left for them and they say I'm doing myself in.

Now list any conflicts you see arising among the various social settings of your life.

EXERCISE 4: Assessing the impact of the larger organizations and
            institutions of society on your life

(1) Here is a list of some of the larger organizations and institutions
that might, directly or indirectly, affect your life and with which you
may have some concerns.

* newspapers   * federal government and its agencies
* television   * state government and its agencies
* the economy   * local government and its agencies
* the institutional church   * the food industry
* the insurance industry   * the mental health system
* the medical industry   * the educational system
* big business   * unions
* law enforcement agencies   * the courts
* transportation   * the energy industry
* professional athletics   * welfare agencies

(2) Indicate any concerns you might have because of the ways in which
any of these institutions are affecting you. Some examples:

* "I think that the sex and violence on TV are harming my children, and
yet they complain bitterly when I restrict what they can see. They say
that other children get to see whatever they want and are not corrupted
by it."
* "I'm getting old and I haven't been able to save any money. I am very
afraid that I'll get sick and that Medicare won't really take care of
me. I keep looking forward to an awful old age. I don't know whether I
should put the little money I have into health insurance for the
elderly. But I saw a TV program the other night in which they talked
about health insurance for the elderly as a racket."
* "I've got a degree in counseling and I can't get a job. The people in
the schools say that I need to be certified as a teacher and have a
school psychologist degree. The people in mental health centers say
they are hiring only social workers. Government cuts mean that service
people are being laid off. No one yet has tried to find out whether I'm
good at my profession or not. I feel I'm being done in by the politics
of the whole situation."

     List any concerns you have that are related to the larger
organizations and institutions that are affecting your life:

EXERCISE 5: Assessing life skills

Sometimes people develop problems or fail to manage them because they do not have the kinds of life skills needed to handle developmental tasks and to invest themselves effectively in the social systems of life. For instance, a young married couple finds that they don't have the communication skills needed to talk to each other reasonably about the problems they encounter during the first couple of years of marriage.

Again, this exercise is a checklist designed to help you get in touch with both your resources and possible areas of deficit. Listed below are various groups of skills needed to undertake the tasks of everyday living. Rate yourself on each skill. The rating system is as follows:

5. I have a very high level of this skill.
4. I have a moderately high level of this skill.
3. From what I can judge, I am about average in this skill.
2. I have some moderate deficit in this skill.
1. I have a serious deficit in this skill.

You are also asked to rate how important each skill is in your eyes. Use the following scale.

5. For me this skill is very important.
4. For me this skill is of moderate importance.
3. For me this skill has average importance.
2. For me this skill is rather unimportant.
1. For me this skill is completely unimportant.

Area A: Body-related skills

	Level	Importance
* Knowing how to put together nutritional meals.	___	___
* Knowing how to control weight.	___	___
* Knowing how to keep fit through exercise.	___	___
* Knowing how to maintain basic body hygiene.	___	___
* Basic grooming skills.	___	___
* Knowing what to do when everyday health problems such as colds and minor accidents occur.	___	___
* Skills related to sexual expression.	___	___
* Athletic skills.	___	___
* Aesthetic skills such as dancing.	___	___

Other body-related skills:

* _____   ___ ___

* _____   ___ ___

* _____   ___ ___

Area B: Learning and Learning-How-to-Learn Skills

* Knowing how to read well.   _____ _____
* Knowing how to write clearly.   _____ _____
* Knowing basic mathematics.   _____ _____
* Knowing how to learn and study efficiently.   _____ _____
* Knowing something about the use of computers.   _____ _____
* Knowing how to see current issues in historical   _____ _____
perspective.
* Knowing something about basic statistics.   _____ _____
* Knowing how to use a library.   _____ _____
* Knowing how to find information I need.   _____ _____

Other learning and learning-how-to-learn skills.

* _____   _____ _____

* _____   _____ _____

* _____   _____ _____

Area C: Skills Related to Values

* Knowing how to clarify my own values.   _____ _____
* Knowing how to identify the values of others   _____ _____
who have a significant relationship to me.
* Knowing how to identify the values being "pushed" _____ _____
by the social systems to which I belong.
* Knowing how to construct and reconstruct my own   _____ _____
    set of values.

Other value-related skills:

* _____   _____ _____

* _____   _____ _____

* _____   _____ _____

Area D: Self-Management Skills

* Knowing how to plan and set realistic goals.   _____ _____
* Problem-solving or problem-management skills.   _____ _____
* Decision-making skills.   _____ _____
* Knowing and being able to use basic principles of _____ _____
behavior such as reinforcement and shaping.
* Knowing how to manage emotions.   _____ _____
* Knowing how to delay gratification.   _____ _____
* Assertiveness: knowing how to get my needs met   _____ _____
while respecting the legitimate needs of others.

Other self-management skills:

* _____ ____ ____

* _____ ____ ____

* _____ ____ ____

Area E: Communication Skills

* The ability to speak before a group.   ____ ____
* The ability to listen to others actively.   ____ ____
* The ability to understand others.   ____ ____
* The ability to communicate understanding to others ____ ____
(empathy).
* The ability to challenge others reasonably. ____ ____
* The ability to provide useful information to others. ____ ____
* The ability to explore with another person what is   ____ ____
happening in my relationship to him or her.

Other communication skills:

* _____ ____ ____

* _____ ____ ____

* _____ ____ ____

Area F: Skills Related to Small Groups

* Knowing how to be an effective active member of   ____ ____
a small group.
* Knowing how to design and organize a group.   ____ ____
* Knowing how to lead a small group.   ____ ____
* Team-building skills.   ____ ____

Other small-group skills:

* _____ ____ ____

* _____ ____ ____

* _____ ____ ____

Area G: Organization Involvement and Development Skills

* The ability to be a contributing member of larger   ____ ____
organizations or institutions.
* Managerial skills.   ____ ____
* Consultation skills.   ____ ____
* Conflict management and negotiation skills. ____ ____
* Organizational design skills.   ____ ____
* The ability to organize efforts to change organi-   ____ ____
zations or institutions.

* Community (neighborhood) development skills. ____ ____
* The skills of political involvement. ____ ____

Other organization-involvement skills:

* _____ ____ ____

* _____ ____ ____

* _____ ____ ____

Identify any skills deficits that are associated with the problems or concerns you have discovered so far. Indicate the skill and what problem or concern it relates to.

_____

_____

_____

_____

_____

_____

What kinds of skills do you think you need to become better at, not just to handle your own problems more effectively, but to be an effective counselor?

_____

_____

_____

_____

_____

_____

_____

_____

_____

_____

EXERCISE 6: A sentence-completion assessment of problems

Exercises 6 and 7 deal with sentence completions. Do them quickly.
They may help you expand in more specific ways what you have learned
about yourself in preceding exercises.

1. My biggest problem is

2. I'm quite concerned about

3. One of my other problems is

4. Something I do that gives me trouble is

5. Something I fail to do that gets me into trouble is

6. The social setting of life I find most troublesome is

7. The most frequent negative feelings in my life are

8. They take place when

9. The person I have most trouble with is

10. What I find most troublesome in this relationship is

11. Life would be better if

12. I tend to do myself in when I

13. I don't cope very well with

14. What sets me most on edge is

15. I get anxious when

16. A value I fail to put into practice is

17. I'm afraid to

18. I wish I

19. I wish I didn't

20. What others dislike most about me is

21. What I don't seem to handle well is

22. I don't seem to have the skills I need in order to

23. A problem that keeps coming back is

24. If I could change just one thing in myself it would be

EXERCISE 7: A sentence-completion assessment of strengths

1. One thing I like about myself is

2. One thing others like about me is

3. One thing I do very well is

4. A recent problem I've handled very well is

5. When I'm at my best I

6. I'm glad that I

7. Those who know me are glad that I

8. A compliment that has been paid to me recently is

9. A value that I try hard to practice is

10. An example of my caring about others is

11. People can count on me to

12. They say I did a good job when I

13. Something I'm handling better this year than last is

14. One thing that I've overcome is

15. A good example of my ability to manage my life is

16. I'm best with people when

17. One goal I'm presently working toward is

18. A recent temptation that I managed to overcome was

19. I pleasantly surprised myself when I

20. I think that I have the guts to

21. If I had to say one good thing about myself I'd say that I

22. One way I successfully control my emotions is

23. One way in which I am very dependable is

24. One important thing I intend to do within two months is

TASK 2: FOCUSING AND INITIAL PROBLEM EXPLORATION

Section 1: Focusing:
Choosing Issues, Problems, or Concerns to Explore

In counseling interviews clients often enough reveal a number of different problems and concerns, and it is up to you to help them decide what they would like to deal with first. In a similar way, now that you have used a number of assessment-oriented exercises to identify some of your concerns, it is time to decide which issues you would like to deal with during the training process.

EXERCISE 8: Choosing issues and concerns to explore

(1) First of all, merely list some of the concerns you have discovered in doing the assessment exercises.

(2) Next, apply the criteria listed below--criteria you can use with clients to help them choose or focus on an issue or concern that they want to address--to each item on the list you have just made.

* Severity or urgency. Is this an issue that needs more or less immediate attention because of the distress it causes you or others and/or because of its frequency or uncontrollability?

* Importance. Is this an issue that's important to you, important enough to discuss and act on?

* Timing. Is this a problem that, in your estimation, can be managed at this time with the resources you have available?

* Complexity. Is this concern a manageable part of a larger or more complex problem situation? Can it be divided into more manageable parts?

* Promise of success. Is this a good problem or part of a problem to begin with since it seems that you can handle it relatively easily with some reasonable assurance of success?

* Spread effect. Is this the kind of problem which, if handled, might lead to improvement in other areas of your life?

* Control. Is this a problem the management of which is under your control? To manage it more effectively do you have to act or do others have to act?

* Cost effectiveness. Is it worth trying to deal with this concern, that is, do the benefits of handling it outweigh the costs in terms of time and effort?

* Willingness. Is this a concern or problem that you are willing to discuss with the members of your training group? Might you be willing to discuss it when you become more comfortable with the members of the group?

* Substance. Is this issue worthwhile discussing? Is it capable of being developed over a number of sessions? On the other hand, is it too serious to be discussed now and in this setting?

(3) With these criteria in mind, review the concerns you have just listed and indicate five concerns or problem areas of some substance which you would be willing to explore when you take the role of client in your training group.

a. _____

_____

_____

b. _____

_____

c. _____

_____

_____

d. _____

_____

_____

e. _____

_____

_____

Section 2: Initial Problem Exploration
Skills Needed To Help Clients Clarify Problems and Concerns

The exercises in this section relate to the skills you need to interview clients and help them explore and clarify the problems, issues, and concerns they come with. The skills dealt with in this section are physical attending, listening, primary-level accurate empathy, and probing.

I. Exercises in Physical Attending

Your body sends out nonverbal messages to your clients. The purpose of these exercises is to make you aware of the different kinds of messages you can send because of your posture. It is important that what you say in your words to your clients is reinforced rather than muddled or contradicted by the nonverbal messages sent by your body.

Before doing these exercises, review the material on attending. Recall especially the basic elements of physical attending summarized by the acronym SOLER:

S--facing the other person SQUARELY can say that you are available to work with him or her.

O--adopting an OPEN posture can say that you are open to the other and nondefensive.

L--LEANING toward the other at times can underscore your listening and responding and tell the other you are with him or her.

E--good EYE contact that avoids staring can tell the other of your interest in him or her.

R--remaining relatively RELAXED while being with the other fully can speak of your competence and help the other relax also.

EXERCISE 9: Experiencing nonattending in the group conversation

1. All the members of the training group (six to eight people) meet
    in a circle for a group discussion.
2. A topic of conversation related to the training process is chosen
    (for instance, the fears or misgivings people have as they are about
    to enter training).
3. All but one or two of the members maintain good attending posture.
    The other one or two violate the SOLER suggestions by slouching and
    so forth. However, they do participate verbally in the discussion.
4. After about four or five minutes the conversation is stopped and the
    reactions of both attenders and nonattenders are discussed. For
    instance, how did you react to a member who was verbally present but
    nonverbally absent.

EXERCISE 10: Relating intensity of physical attending to the substance
    of the conversation

1. Each person in the training group finds a partner.
2. They both assume a position of intense attending, including sitting
    close, facing each other squarely, maintaining good eye contact, and
    leaning forward.
3. They then talk about the weather or some other trivial subject for
    about a minute or two.
4. The conversation is stopped and they talk about whatever incongruity
    they felt between the attending position and the subject discussed.
    They discuss the proposition: The SOLER attending suggestions make
    sense only if what is being discussed merits that kind of intensity.

EXERCISE 11: Observing and giving feedback on nonverbal and
    voice-related behavior

    Physical attending has two functions: (1) it is a sign to others
that you are actively involved and working with them, and (2) it helps
you be an _active listener_ (that is, physical attending, when carried out
appropriately, can aid psychological attending).
    In this exercise you are given an opportunity to observe the
nonverbal and voice-related behavior of two people talking to each other
(voice-related behavior refers to the way people use their voices in
communicating and includes such things as tone of voice, loudness, pitch,
speed in talking, stumbling over words, grunts, signs, and so on).
Nonverbal behavior serves to underscore or "punctuate" verbal messages in
various ways.

1. Divide into groups of four with members A, B, C, and D.
2. A and B have a five-minute conversation in which they discuss what
    they like or don't like about their interpersonal styles. This
    conversation, as much as possible, should be a dialogue (that is,
    they should talk to and respond to each other and not just give
    speeches).

3. Members C and D act as observers. They take written notes on A and B's attending and on their voice-related behavior.

4. After about five minutes, the conversation is stopped and C and D give A and B feedback, using the SOLER suggestions as a basis for the feedback. <u>A caution</u>: The purpose of this exercise is to give you an opportunity to observe nonverbal attending and voice-related behavior. At this stage, it is best to note the variety of such behavior without interpreting it. While brief interpretations cannot be avoided altogether, they should in no way become the focus of the feedback session. Your ability to interpret such behavior will grow with your experience.

5. After a four- or five-minute feedback session is completed, then the entire process is repeated with C and D as the speakers and A and B the observers.

Here are some typical feedback statements:

* "Most of the time you spoke very quickly, in spurts. It gave me a feeling of tension or nervousness."
* "You sat very still throughout the conversation. Your hands remained folded in your lap, and there was practically no bodily movement."
* "When you talked about being a very sensitive person, one who is easily hurt, your voice became very soft and you stumbled over your words a bit."
* "You tapped your left foot almost constantly."
* "You put your hand to your mouth a great deal. It distracted me."
* "When your partner began talking about being shy, you leaned back and even moved your chair back a little. It looked like you were giving her room to speak."
* "You broke eye contact a great deal when you were talking about yourself, but not when you were listening to your partner."

II. <u>Exercises in Listening and Concreteness of Expression</u>

Assessment models such as the people-in-systems model help you listen to and organize the <u>content</u> of the client's disclosures. However, since problem situations cannot usually be managed more effectively until they are clarified, it is also necessary for you to listen to <u>how concretely or specifically</u> the client is talking about his or her problems in living. A problem situation or some part of it is clear if it is spelled out in terms of <u>specific experiences, specific behaviors, and specific feelings and emotions in specific situations</u>. As indicated in the text, each of these may be overt (external, capable of being seen by someone other than the client) or covert (internal, capable of being seen only by the client). Therefore, when you listen to clients, you can ask yourself how specifically they are talking about their overt and covert experiences, behaviors, and feelings.

<u>An experience</u>: something clients describe as <u>happening to</u> them:
  <u>Overt</u>: "He hit me."
  <u>Covert</u>: "I can't stop thinking of her."

A <u>behavior</u>: something clients <u>do or fail to do</u>.
   <u>Overt</u>: "I spend about three hours every night in some bar."
   <u>Covert</u>: "Before she comes over I plan everything I'm going to say."
A <u>feeling or emotion</u>: the <u>affect</u> associated with experiences or behaviors.
   <u>Overt</u> (expressed): "I got very angry and shouted at her."
   <u>Covert</u> (felt, but not expressed): "I was delighted that he failed, but I didn't let on."

This schema will be used in three ways in this book of exercises:
1. To help you perceive how concretely (or nonconcretely) a client is talking.
2. To help you speak more concretely about your own experiences, behaviors, and feelings.
3. To enable you, through the use of probes (in the section on probes), to help clients explore problem situations more thoroughly.

EXERCISE 12: Speaking concretely about experiences

In this exercise, you are asked to speak of some of your experiences--first vaguely, then concretely. Read the following examples.

Example 1

* <u>Vague statement of experience</u>: "I'm sometimes less efficient because of a physical condition."
* <u>Concrete statement of the same experience</u>: "I get migraine headaches about once a week. They make me extremely sensitive to light and usually cause severe pain. I often get so sick that I throw up. They happen more often when I'm tense or under a lot of pressure. For instance, I come away from a visit with my ex-wife with one."

Example 2

* <u>Vague statement of experience</u>: "People pick on me."
* <u>Concrete statement of the same experience</u>: "My classmates ridicule me for being overweight. They call me 'Fatso,' 'Porky,' and 'Tubby.' They don't invite me to their parties. They even say that they don't invite me because I'd eat too much."

In the spaces below, deal with three instances of your own experience. Stick to experiences rather than behaviors or feelings. If possible, deal with experiences that are of some concern to you and that could relate to the quality of your helping. Remember that experiences become concrete if they are specific and are related to specific situations.

1. <u>Vague.</u> _____

_____

Concrete. _____

_____

_____

_____

_____

2. Vague. _____

_____

Concrete. _____

_____

_____

_____

_____

3. Vague. _____

_____

Concrete: _____

_____

_____

_____

_____

EXERCISE 13: Speaking concretely about your behavior

In this exercise, you are asked to speak about some of your behavior (what you do or fail to do)--first vaguely, then concretely. Choose behavior that might affect your role as helper. Read the following examples.

Example 1

* Vague statement of behavior: "I tend to be fickle."
* Concrete statement of the same experience: "I often make three or more social arrangements for the weekend and then, when the weekend comes, I choose the one or two that suit me the best at the time. This means that I leave others stranded. But I'm a smooth talker and, if feathers get ruffled, I can usually smooth them.

Example 2

* <u>Vague statement of behavior</u>: "I don't treat my wife right."
* <u>Concrete statement of the same behavior</u>: "When I come home from work, I read the paper and watch some TV. I don't talk much to my wife except a bit at supper. I don't share the little things that went on in my day. Neither do I encourage her to talk about what happened to her. Still, if I feel like having sex later, I expect her to hop in bed with me willingly."

In the spaces below, deal with three instances of your own behavior. Stick mostly to behaviors rather than descriptions of experiences or feelings. Try to choose situations and behaviors that could be relevant to your interpersonal or helping style.

1. <u>Vague</u>. _____

_____

<u>Concrete</u>. _____

_____

_____

_____

_____

2. <u>Vague</u>. _____

_____

<u>Concrete</u>. _____

_____

_____

_____

_____

3. <u>Vague</u>. _____

_____

<u>Concrete</u>. _____

_____

_____

_____

_____

EXERCISE 14: Speaking concretely about feelings and emotions

     Feelings and emotions arise because of what you experience and what
you do. Therefore, it is unrealistic to talk about feelings without
relating them to experiences or behaviors. However, in this exercise try
to emphasize the feelings rather than the experiences or behaviors to
which they relate. Read the following examples.

Example 1

* Vague statement of feelings: "Training groups are sometimes difficult
for me."
* Concrete statement of the same feelings: "I feel hesitant and
embarrassed whenever I want to give feedback to other trainees,
especially if it is in any way negative. When the time comes, my heart
beats faster and my palms sweat. I feel like everyone is staring at me."

Example 2

* Vague statement of feelings: "My relationship with my mother bothers
me sometimes."
* Concrete statement of the same feelings: "I feel guilty and depressed
whenever my mother calls and implies that she's lonely. It's like a
burden on me the rest of the day, especially if I can't get over there."

     In the spaces below, deal with three instances of your own feelings.
Try to focus on feelings that you have some trouble in handling or which
could interfere with your role as helper.

1. Vague. _____

_____

     Concrete. _____

_____

_____

_____

_____

2. Vague. _____

_____

Concrete. _____

_____

_____

_____

_____

3. Vague. _____

_____

Concrete. _____

_____

_____

_____

_____

_____

EXERCISE 15: Speaking concretely about experiences, behaviors, and
    feelings together

In this exercise, you are asked to bring together all three elements--
specific experiences, specific behaviors, and specific feelings--in
talking about some personal issue that concerns you. Study the following
examples.

Example 1

* Vague statement: "I'm not as mature sexually as I'd like to be."
* Concrete statement: "I'm afraid of women, especially women who
come on strong, even women who are just plain assertive. My sexual
life consists almost entirely of fantasies and masturbation. In these
fantasies I am the dominant male and women make no demands on me. They
are submissive and are there just for my sexual needs. I'm ashamed to
say that I get a kick out of it. Sometimes I'm obsessed by thoughts like
this. For the present it seems to satisfy my sexual needs. Some women
are attracted to me, but I make excuses why I can't go out. I'm really
scared, but I hide it by being offhand. I intimate that I have a life
full of women someplace else. So I feel phony when I'm around women.
And I feel guilty when I take any kind of serious look at myself as a
sexual person. I try not to think much about it."

Pick out the experiences, behaviors, and feelings in this example.

Example 2

* <u>Vague statement</u>: "Sometimes I'm a rather overly sensitive and spiteful person."
* <u>Concrete statement</u>: "I do not take criticism well. When I receive almost any kind of negative feedback, I usually smile and seem to shrug it off, but inside I begin to pout. Also deep inside I put the person who gave me the feedback on a 'list.' I say to myself that that person is going to pay for what he or she did. For instance, two weeks ago in the training group I received some negative feedback from you, Cindy. I felt angry and hurt because I thought you were my 'friend.' Since then I've tried to see what mistakes you make here. I've been looking for an opportunity to get back at you. I've even felt bad because I haven't been able to catch you. I'm ashamed of myself as I say all this."

Pick out the experiences, behaviors, and feelings in this example.

Next talk about two situations in terms of your own experiences, behaviors, and feelings. Again try to deal with themes that relate to your potential effectiveness as a helper.

1. <u>Vague</u>. _____

_____

<u>Concrete</u>. _____

_____

_____

_____

_____

_____

_____

_____

_____

2. <u>Vague</u>. _____

_____

<u>Concrete</u>. _____

_____

_____

_____

_____

_____

_____

_____

_____

_____

_____

III.   Exercises in Primary-Level Accurate Empathy

As you know from your review of the text material on primary-level accurate empathy, this skill is useful both in (1) establishing and developing a good working relationship with your client and (2) as a way of helping the client explore his or her problem situation more thoroughly.

The basic formula for primary-level accurate empathy is:

"You feel. . . ."--here indicate the right family of emotion and the right intensity . . .

"because . . ."--here indicate the experiences and/or behaviors that give rise to the feelings.

An example.

*   You feel hurt because she left without calling you (an experience).
*   You feel annoyed with yourself because you didn't do anything about it (a behavior).
*   You feel guilty because she put her pride aside and asked you directly for help and you didn't even answer her (experience and behavior).

A.   The Feelings and Emotions Component of Empathy

EXERCISE 16: Expanding your facility in naming feelings and emotions

Feelings and emotions can be identified in a variety of ways:

*   by single words:

    I feel good.
    I'm depressed.

I feel abandoned.
I'm delighted.
I feel trapped.
I'm angry.

* by different kinds of phrases:

I'm sitting on top of the world.
I feel down in the dumps.
I feel left in the lurch.
I feel tip top.
My back's up against the wall.
I'm really steaming.

* by what is implied in a behavioral statement   (what action I feel
like taking):

I feel like giving up. (implied emotion: despair)
I feel like hugging you. (implied emotion: joy)
I feel like smashing him in the face. (implied emotion: severe anger)
Now that it's over, I feel like dancing in the streets. (implied
    emotion: relief)

* by what is implied in experiences that are revealed:

I feel I'm being dumped on. (implied feeling: anger)
I feel I'm being stereotyped. (implied feeling: resentment)
I feel I'm first on her list. (implied feeling: joy)
I feel I'm going to get it this time. (implied feeling: fear)

Note here that the implication could be spelled out:

I feel angry because I'm being dumped on.
I resent the fact that I'm being sterotyped.
I feel great because I believe I'm first on her list.
I feel apprehensive because I think I'm going to get it this time.

A number of situations involving different kinds of feelings and
emotions are listed below. Picture yourself talking to this person and
you are asked to express them in the ways just described. Here is an
example.

Joy: This person has just been given a job she really wanted.
    Single word: You're happy.
    A phrase: You're on cloud nine.
    A you-feel-like statement: You feel like going out and celebrating.
    Experiential statement: You feel you got what you deserve.

Now express the following feelings and emotions in three different ways.

1. Joy. This person is about to go to her daughter's graduation from
college.

_____

_____

2. <u>Anger</u>. This woman has just had her purse stolen.

_____

_____

_____

3. <u>Anxiety</u>. This person is waiting the results of medical tests.

_____

_____

_____

4. <u>Shame, embarrassment</u>. People have just found out that this person has a criminal record.

_____

_____

_____

5. <u>Defeated</u>. This person has just lost a custody case for her children.

_____

_____

_____

6. <u>Confusion</u>. Someone has just told this person that she loves him but that she doesn't want to spend any time with him.

_____

_____

_____

7. <u>Guilt, regret</u>. This person has been unfair to his children.

_____

_____

_____

8. <u>Depression</u>. This person has just been abandoned by his wife.

_____

_____

_____

9. <u>Contentment</u>. This person has just finished a very difficult project successfully.

_____

_____

_____

10. <u>Pressure</u>. This person's boss has just told him that the project must be finished by the end of the week or else.

_____

_____

_____

11. <u>Distress</u>. This person is developing a migraine headache.

_____

_____

_____

12. <u>Boredom</u>. This person is talking about her job on the assembly line.

_____

_____

_____

13. <u>Hope</u>. This person has been told that there might be a cure for her child's illness.

_____

_____

_____

14. <u>Low physical energy</u>. This person is talking about having to work

two jobs to support her children.

_____

_____

_____

15. <u>Despair</u>. This person has just found out that he is being laid off
for the third time this year.

_____

_____

_____

EXERCISE 17: A review of feelings and emotions

     If you are to help others clarify their feelings and emotions, you
should first be familiar with your own emotional states. In a book
called <u>How Do You Feel</u>?, edited by John Wood (Englewood Cliffs, New
Jersey: Prentice-Hall, Inc., 1974), Wood and others describe in detail
their own experiences of a wide range of emotions. These emotional
states are listed below. You are asked to describe what you feel when
you feel these emotions. Describe what you feel as <u>concretely</u> as
possible: How does your body react? What happens inside you? What do
you feel like doing? Consider the following examples.

Example 1

<u>Accepted</u>: When I feel accepted,

     I feel warm inside.
     I feel safe.
     I feel free to be myself.
     I feel like sitting back and relaxing.
     I feel I can let my guard down.
     I feel like sharing myself.
     I feel some of my fears easing away.
     I feel at home.
     I feel at peace.
     I feel my loneliness drifting away.

Example 2

<u>Scared</u>: When I feel scared,

     My mouth dries up.
     My bowels become loose.
     There are butterflies in my stomach.
     I feel like running away.
     I feel very uncomfortable.

I feel the need to talk to someone.
I turn in on myself.
I feel useless.
I'm unable to concentrate.
I feel very vulnerable.
I feel like whining or crying.

In order to keep this from becoming just an intellectual exercise, try to picture yourself in situations in which you have actually experienced these emotions. Then write down what you see in your imagination.

1. accepted	11. defensive	22. lonely
2. affectionate	12. disappointed	23. loving
3. afraid	13. free	24. rejected
4. angry	14. frustrated	25. repulsed
5. anxious	15. guilty	26. respect
6. attracted	16. hopeful	27. sad
7. bored	17. hurt	28. satisfied
8. belonging, in community	18. inferior	29. shy
	19. intimate	30. suspicious
9. competitive	20. jealous	31. superior
10. confused	21. joyful	32. trusting

Once you have described how you feel when you feel these emotions, you should have a wider repertory of words, phrases, and statements both to describe your own emotional states and to identify emotional states in others.

EXERCISE 18: An intense emotional experience

Recall an intense emotional experience you would be willing to share with the members of your training group. Write it down as concretely as possible.

Example

Scared: "I was going to Europe last year by plane. The captain told us that it would be a smooth flight. About an hour and a half into the flight, it was as if we hit a brick wall. Bang! For the next three hours we jumped and bumped and dived and swooped up. No one said anything. No announcements from the captain. I was besides myself with fear. People began to get sick. I've never been sick on an airplane, but I began getting sick. But the terror went on and on. It went on that way for over three hours straight. I didn't talk to anyone. I sat frozen in my seat holding on. I was this huge jangle of nerves for over three hours."

Now write out some highly emotional experience you have had. Note that the emotions need not be negative.

_____

_____

_____

_____

_____

_____

_____

_____

_____

_____

_____

_____

Pick a partner, share your experiences, and then spend five to ten minutes talking about them.

EXERCISE 19: Emotions you have some trouble managing

Some people have more difficulty experiencing and expressing emotions than others. Everyone has more difficulty with some emotions than others.

1. Review the list of 32 emotional states found in Exercise 17.
2. Check the emotions you have trouble with.
3. Choose three of them and write a few sentences describing the trouble you have. Be concrete and specific. Note the kinds of specific situations in which you have difficulty.
4. Share your three sets of difficulties, each with a separate partner.
5. Once you have completed the sharing, review the five concerns or problem areas you listed in Exercise 8 and see whether they include at least by implication the difficulties with emotions that you discover in this exercise.

Example

Derryl chooses "hurt" as an emotion he has trouble with. Here are some of the things he has to say about it: "After I get hurt, I often get angry or depressed. It's much easier for me to admit these. Hurt, at least for me, is deeper. I feel that if I admit that I'm hurt it makes me small and weak. I guess I want to appear strong to others all

<u>the time</u>. I'm not sure why admitting vulnerability makes me think I'm weak."

a. Emotion. _____

    Difficulties with it. _____

_____

_____

_____

_____

_____

b. Emotion. _____

    Difficulties with it. _____

_____

_____

_____

_____

_____

c. Emotion. _____

    Difficulties with it. _____

_____

_____

_____

_____

_____

EXERCISE 20: Identifying the feelings of clients

     Now that you have considered feelings and emotions in your own life,
it is time to test your ability to identify emotions that are expressed by
others or implied in what they say.
     Read the following statements; then write down a number of adjectives
or phrases describing how the speaker feels.   Consider the following
example.

Example.

     A twenty-seven year old man is talking to a minister about a visit
with his mother the previous day. "I just don't know what got into me!
She kept nagging me the way she always does, asking me why I don't visit
her more often. As she went on I got more and more angry. (He looks
away from the counselor and looks toward the floor.) I finally began
screaming at her. I told her to get off my case. (He puts his hands
over his face.) I can't believe what I did! I called her a bitch.
(Shaking his head.) I called her a bitch about ten times and then I left
and slammed the door in her face."

How does this person feel?   embarrassed, guilty, ashamed, distraught,
amazed, extremely disappointed with himself, remorseful

Note carefully: This man is talking about his anger, but at the moment
he is feeling and expressing the emotions listed above.

1. A woman, 40, married, no children: "These counseling sessions have
really done me a great deal of good! I enjoy my work more. I actually
look forward to meeting new people. My husband and I are talking more
seriously and decently to each other. There's just so much more freedom
in my life!"

How does this person feel? _____

_____

How intense is the emotion or emotions and how do you know? _____

_____

2. A woman, 53, about to get divorced: "My husband and I just decided
to get a divorce. (Her voice is very soft, her speech is slow,
halting.) I really don't look forward to the legal part of
it--(pause)--to any part of it to tell the truth. I just don't know what
to expect. (She sighs heavily.) I'm well into middle age. I don't
think another marriage is possible. I just don't know what to expect."

How does this person feel? _____

_____

How intense is the emotion or emotions and how do you know? _____

_____

3. A man, 45, with a daughter, 14, who was just hit by a car: "I should
never have allowed my daughter to go to the movies alone. (He keeps
wringing his hands.) I don't know what my wife will say when she gets
home from work. (He grimaces.) She says I'm careless--but being
careless with the kids--that's something else! (He stands up and walks
around.) I almost feel as if I had broken Karen's arm, not the guy in
that car. (He sits down, stares at the floor, keeps tapping his fingers
on the desk.) I don't know."

How does this person feel? _____

_____

How intense is the emotion or emotions and how do you know? _____

_____

4. A woman, 38, unmarried, talking about losing a friend: "My best
friend has just turned her back on me. And I don't even know why! (said
with great emphasis) From the way she acted, I think she has the idea
that I've been talking behind her back. I simply have not! (said with
great emphasis) Damn! This neighborhood is full of spiteful gossips.
She should know that. If she's been listening to those foulmouths who
just want to stir up trouble. . . . She could at least tell me what's
going on."

How does this person feel? _____

_____

How intense is the emotion or emotions and how do you know? _____

_____

5. A senior in high school, 17, talking to his girl friend: "My teacher
told me today that I've done better work than she ever expected. I
always thought I could be good at studies if I applied myself. (He
smiles.) So I tried this semester and it's paid off."

How does this person feel? _____

_____

How intense is the emotion or emotions and how do you know? _____

_____

6. A trainee, 29, speaking to the members of his training group: "I
don't know what to expect in this group. (He speaks hesitatingly.) I've
never been in this kind of group before. From what I've seen so far, I,
well, I get the feeling that you're pros, and I keep watching myself to

see if I'm doing things right. (Sighs heavily.) I'm comparing myself
to what everyone else is doing. I want to get good at this stuff . . .
(pause) . . . but frankly I'm not sure I can make it."

How does this person feel? _____

_____

How intense is the emotion or emotions and how do you know? _____

_____

7. A young women, 19, speaking to a college counselor toward the end of
her second year: "I've been in college almost two years now, and nothing
much has happened. (She speaks listlessly.) The teachers here are only
so-so. I thought they'd be a lot better. At least that's what I heard.
And I can't say much for the social life here. Things go on the same
from day to day, from week to week."

How does this person feel? _____

_____

How intense is the emotion or emotions and how do you know? _____

_____

8. A man, 64, who has been told that he has terminal cancer, speaking to
a medical resident: "Why me? Why me? I'm not even that old! And I
don't smoke or anything like that. (He begins to cry.) Look at me. I
thought I had some guts. I'm just a slobbering mess. Oh God, why
terminal? What are these next months going to be like? (Pause, he stops
crying.) What would you care! I'm just a failure to you guys."

How does this person feel? _____

_____

How intense is the emotion or emotions and how do you know? _____

_____

9. A woman, 42, married, with three children in their early teens
speaking to a church counselor: "Why does my husband keep blaming me for
his trouble with the kids? I'm always in the middle. He complains to me
about them. They complain to me about him. (She looks the counselor
straight in the eye and talks very deliberately.) I could walk out on
the whole thing right now. Who the hell do they think they are?"

What does this person feel? _____

_____

How intense is the emotion or emotions and how do you know? _____

10. A bachelor, 39, speaking to the members of a life-style group to which he has belonged for about a year: "I've finally met a woman who is very genuine and who lets me be myself. I can care deeply about her without making a child out of her. (He is speaking in a soft, steady voice.) And she cares about me without mothering me. I never thought it would happen. (He raises his voice a bit.) Is it actually happening to me? Is it actually happening?"

How does this person feel? _____

_____

How intense is the emotion or emotions and how do you know? _____

_____

11. A girl in her late teens who is serving a two-year term in a reformatory speaking to a probation counselor: (She sits silently for a while and doesn't answer any question the counselor puts to her. Then she shakes her head and looks around the room.) "I don't know what I'm doing here. You're the third counselor they've sent me to--or is it the fourth? It's a waste of time! Why do they keep making me come here? (She looks straight at the counselor.) Let's fold the show right now. Come on, get smart."

How does this person feel? _____

_____

How intense is the emotion or emotions and how do you know? _____

_____

12. A man, 54, talking to a counselor about a situation at work: "I don't know where to turn. They're asking me to do things at work that I just don't think are right. If I don't do them, well, I'll probably be let go. And I don't know where I'm going to get another job at my age in this economy. But if I do what they want me to, I think I could get into trouble, I mean legal trouble. I'd be the fall guy. My head's spinning. I've never had to face anything like this before. Where do I turn?"

How does this person feel? _____

_____

How intense is the emotion or emotions and how do you know? _____

_____

B. The Experiences and Behaviors Component of Accurate Empathy

EXERCISE 21: Identifying feelings and the experiences and behaviors
    underlying these feelings

In this exercise you are asked to identify not only feelings and
emotions but also the key or relevant experiences and behaviors that give
rise to them. The question is: what experiences (what happens to the
client) and what behaviors (what the client does or fails to do)
contribute to the way the client is feeling? In some cases the client's
experience might be key, in some cases his or her behavior, and in some
cases both. Consider the following example.

Example

A seventh-grade boy talking to a teacher he trusts (all this is said
in a halting voice and he does not look at the teacher): "Something
happened yesterday that's bothering me a lot. I was looking out the
window after school. It was late. I saw two of the guys, the bullies,
beating up on one of my best friends. I was afraid to go down. A
coward. I didn't tell anyone, I didn't do anything."

Feelings: ashamed, guilty, down, miserable

Relevant experience: watching a good friend get beat up

Relevant behavior: failing to help his friend

In this case the client's behavior, not helping, seems to be key to
how he is feeling as he talks with the teacher.

1. A young woman talking to a counselor in a center for battered women:
"This is the third time he's beaten me up. I didn't come before because
I still can't believe it! We're married only a year. After we got
married, he began ordering me around in ways he never did before we got
married. He'd get furious if I questioned him. Then he began shoving me
if I didn't do what he wanted fast or right. And I just let him do it!
I just let him do it! (She breaks down and sobs.) And now three
beatings in about four weeks. Oh God, what's happened?"

Feelings: _____

Relevant experience: _____

Relevant behavior: _____

2. A girl, 12, talking to a psychologist at a time when her parents are
involved in a divorce case: "I still want to do something to help, but I
can't. I just can't! They won't let me. When they would fight and get
real mean and were screaming at each other, I'd run and try to get in
between them. One or the other would push me away. They wouldn't pay any
attention to me at all. They're still pushing me away. They don't care

how I think or feel or what happens to me! My mother tells me that kids should stay out of things like this."

Feelings: _____

Relevant experience: _____

Relevant behavior: _____

2. A man, 25, in a counselor training group talking to the trainer: "I've been sitting here watching you give Peggy feedback. You're doing it very well. But I'm also saying to myself, 'Why isn't he that helpful and that careful with me?' I want the same kind of feedback, but you don't say much to me at all. I'm as active as anyone else in the group. I volunteer to act as both counselor and client. I don't know why you pass me by."

Feelings: _____

Relevant experience: _____

Relevant behavior: _____

3. A woman, 35, with two children, one four, one six, whose husband has deserted them talking to a social worker: "He's not sending me any money. I don't even know where he is. They're asking me for the rent and telling me that I'll be out if I don't come up with it. I've been to two different agencies and filled out all sorts of forms, but I don't have any money or food stamps yet. I've been getting food from my mother, but she's really got next to nothing. What am I supposed to do? I'll work, but who's to take care of the kids. I asked all around and there's no day-care center anywhere near here."

Feelings: _____

Relevant experience: _____

Relevant behavior: _____

4. A man, 53, talking to a counselor a few months after the sudden death of his wife. His two children are married and living in distant towns: "I miss her so. The house seems so empty. I work alone on computer programs. There's no one I talk to at work. Now there's no one at home. I walk around the house thinking of how I was with her in each room. At night sometimes I sit in the dark thinking of nothing. We had few friends, so no one calls. And I haven't seen either of the kids since the funeral."

Feelings: _____

Relevant experience: _____

Relevant behavior: _____

5. A woman, 63, in a hospital dying of cancer, talking to a member of the pastoral counseling staff: "I can understand it from my children, but not from my husband. I know I'm dying. But he comes here with a brave smile every day, hiding what <u>he</u> feels. We never talk about my dying. I know he's trying to protect me, but it's so unreal. I don't tell him that his constant cheerfulness and his refusal to talk about my sickness are actually painful to me. (She shakes her head.) I'm being careful of <u>him</u>!"

Feelings: _____

Relevant experience: _____

Relevant behavior: _____

6. A freshman in college talking to a counselor toward the end of his first year: "One week I find myself studying hard, working on the school paper, going to a talk on foreign affairs. The next week I'm boozing it up, looking around for a hot sex partner, and playing cards all day with the boys. It's like being two different people who don't even know each other! I like being in college, away from home and all that. But when I'm here I don't know what I want."

Feelings: _____

Relevant experience: _____

Relevant behavior: _____

7. Man, 70, arrested for stealing funds from the company where he has worked for 25 years, talking to his lawyer: "To tell you the truth, it's probably a good thing I've been caught. I've been stealing on and off for the last five or six years. It's been a game. It soaked up my energies, my attention, distracted me from thinking about getting old. Now I'm saying to myself: 'You old fool, what're you running from?' I've been forcing myself to try to make sense out of my life. You're probably thinking: 'It's about time, old guy.' I'm thinking it's as good a time as any."

Feelings: _____

Relevant experience: _____

Relevant behavior: _____

8. Woman, 37, married, with an unwanted pregnancy; she has two children, one in the seventh and one in the eighth grade; she is talking to another woman, her closest friend: "Ellen, I just don't know what to do. I've talked to my pastor, but I knew what he was going to say. He wasn't much help at all. Oh, God, I don't want another child! Not now! A couple of people I know just assume I'll have an abortion. That's what they'd do. I won't have an abortion, I just won't. But I don't want to have to restructure my life. I've had my children!"

Feelings: _____

Relevant experience: _____

Relevant behavior: _____

9. A boy, 11, who has been sexually abused by an older male relative,
talking to a counselor (he speaks is a jerky, agitated voice): "I liked
him a lot. He was always nice to me. He took me to ball games. He gave
me spending money. I mean he was not some kind of jerk. He was really
kind. He was drunk when it happened. I trusted him. I wasn't even sure
what was happening. I don't know what to think. Maybe I shouldn't have
said anything. He looked so awful when I saw him yesterday. I <u>had</u> to
say something, didn't I?"

Feelings: _____

Relevant experience: _____

Relevant behavior: _____

10. A minister who has been having an affair with one of his parishioners
talking to another minister: "I've never known anyone like her before.
It was as if it didn't make any difference that both of us were married.
I've never experienced such strong emotion. I can tell myself exactly
what I should do. But I don't do it. We avoid talking about where all
this is going to lead. I know in the back of my mind that my family and
career and all that are on the line, but I keep it pushed back. There's
doom on the horizon, but the present is so damn full!"

Feelings: _____

Relevant experience: _____

Relevant behavior: _____

    C. <u>Empathy: Integrating Feelings with Experiences and Behavior</u>

<u>EXERCISE 22: Responding to the client with primary-level empathy</u>

In this exercise you are asked to do two things: (a) use the "you
feel . . . because . . ." formula to respond to the client; (b) recast
your response in your own words while still identifying both feelings and
the experience and/or behavior that underlies the feelings. Consider the
following example.

Example

Married woman, 31, talking to a counselor about her marriage: "I can't
believe it! You know when Tom and I were here last week we made a
contract that said that he would be home for supper every evening and on

time. Well, he came home on time every day this past week. I never dreamed that he would live up to his part of the bargain so completely!"

Formula: "You <u>feel</u> great <u>because</u> he really stuck to his word."

Nonformula: "He performed beyond your expectations. Now that's a very pleasant surprise!"

In this nonformula response, identify the feeling component and the experience/behavior component.

Now imagine yourself listening intently to each of the people quoted below. First use the "You feel . . . because . . ." formula; then use your own words. Try to make the second response sound as natural (as much like yourself) as possible. After you use your own words, check to see if you have both a "you feel" part and a "because" part in your response.

1. Man, 40, talking about his invalid mother: "I know she's using her present illness to control me. How could a 'good' son refuse any of her requests at a time like this? (He pounds his fist on the arm of his chair.) But it's all part of a pattern. She's used one thing or another to control me all my life. If I let things go on like this, she'll make me feel responsible for her death!"

Formula: _____

_____

Your own words: _____

_____

2. Woman, 25, talking about her current boyfriend: "I can't quite figure him out. (She pauses, shakes her head slowly, and then speaks quite slowly.) I just can't figure out whether he really cares about me, or if he's just trying to get me into bed. I've been burned before; I don't want to get burned again."

Formula: _____

_____

Your own words: _____

_____

3. Businessman, 38, talking to a close associate: "I really don't know what my boss wants. I don't know what he thinks of me. He tells me I'm doing fine even though I don't think that I'm doing anything special. Then he blows up over nothing at all. I keep asking myself if there's something wrong with me, I mean, that I don't see what's getting him to act the way he does. I'm beginning to wonder if this is the right job for me."

Formula: _____

_____

Your own words: _____

_____

4. Woman, 73, in the hospital with a broken hip: "When you get old, you
have to expect things like this to happen. It could have been much
worse. When I lie here, I keep thinking of the people in the world who
are a lot worse off than I am. I'm not a complainer. Oh, I'm not saying
that this is fun or that the people in this place give you the best
service--who does these days?--but it's a good thing that these
hospitals exist."

Formula: _____

_____

Your own words: _____

_____

5. Seventh-grade girl to teacher, outside class: "My classmates don't
like me, and right now I don't like them! Why do they have to be so
mean? They make fun of me--well, they make fun of my clothes. My family
can't afford what some of those snots wear. Gee, they don't have to like
me, but I wish they'd stop making fun of me."

Formula: _____

_____

Your own words: _____

_____

6. High school counselor, 41, talking to a colleague: "Sometimes I
think I'm living a lie. I don't have any interest in high school kids
anymore. So when they come into my office, I don't really do much to
help them. Most of them and their problems bore me. But I've been here
now for twelve years. I like living around here. I try half-heartedly
to work up some interest, but I don't get far."

Formula: _____

_____

Your own words: _____

_____

7. Man, 35, who has not been feeling well talking to a friend of his who
is a nurse: "I'm going into the hospital tomorrow for some tests. I

think they suspect an ulcer. (He fidgets.) But nobody has told me exactly what kind of tests. I'm supposed to take these enemas and not eat anything after supper this evening. I've heard rumors about these kinds of tests, but I'm not really sure what they're like."

Formula: _____

_____

Your own words: _____

_____

8. Graduate student, 25, to advisor: "I have two term papers due tomorrow. I'm giving a report in class this afternoon. My husband is down with the flu. And now I find out that a special committee wants to 'talk' with me about my 'progress' in the program."

Formula: _____

_____

Your own words: _____

_____

9. Woman, 43, talking to a counselor in a rape crisis center: "It was all I could do to come here. A friend told me to call the police. And then I'd become one of those stories you read in the paper everyday! Or they'd be asking me all sorts of questions. Ugh! I just want to forget it. I don't want to keep reliving it over and over again."

Formula: _____

_____

Your own words: _____

_____

10. Female high school student, 17, talking to a male counselor about an unexpected pregnancy: "I, well, I don't think I can talk about it here. (Pause) You being a man and all that. (Pause) What happens between me and my boyfriend and me and my family--well, that's all very personal. I don't talk to strangers about personal things."

Formula: _____

_____

Your own words: _____

_____

EXERCISE 23: Accurate empathy with contrasting emotions

Clients sometimes talk about contrasting emotions and experiences. Responding empathically to them means communicating an understanding of the contrast or conflict. Consider the following example.

Example

A woman, 32, talking to a counselor about a possible abortion: "I'm going back and forth, back and forth. I say to myself, 'Okay, I'll have the abortion,' then that seems to handle my reluctance to have another child and it means that Bill [her husband] will be relieved. I don't especially want another child, but he's totally opposed to it. So an abortion seems to be a way out. But the very next moment I begin thinking about the abortion itself or, even worse, how I'll feel about myself afterwards, and then I'm back at square one."

Identify the conflict or dilemma: An abortion might solve some problems, but it might also create some new ones.

Formula: "In one way, you feel relieved when you think about having the abortion, because this will solve some very practical problems for you and Bill, but almost at the same time you feel apprehensive because you're not at all sure what having an abortion is going to do to you."

Nonformula: "You're caught in the middle. Having an abortion might well solve some serious problems, and that would be a relief. But you're asking yourself, 'What price am I going to pay?' You seem to fear that it could be too high."

1. Factory worker, 30: "Work is okay. I do make a good living, and both my family and I like the money. My wife and I are both from poor homes, and we're living much better than we did when we were growing up. But the work I do is the same thing day after day. I may not be the world's brightest person, but there's a lot more to me than I use on those machines."

The conflict: Work is good, but work is also bad. _____

Formula: _____

_____

_____

Your own words: _____

_____

_____

2. Mental hospital patient, 54, who has spent five years in the hospital; he is talking to the members of an ongoing therapy group; some

of the members have been asking him what he's doing to get out: "To tell
the truth, I like it here. So why are so many people here so damn eager
to see me out. Is it a crime because I feel comfortable here? (Pause,
then in a more conciliatory voice.) I know you're all interested in me.
I see that you care. But do I have to please you by doing something I
don't want to do?"

The conflict: _____

_____

Formula: _____

_____

_____

Your own words: _____

_____

_____

3. Juvenile probation officer to colleague: "These kids drive me up the
wall. Sometimes I think I'm really stupid for doing this kind of work.
They taunt me. They push me as far as they can. To some of them I'm
just another 'pig.' But every time I think of quitting--and this gets me--
I know I'd miss the work and even miss the kids one way or another. When
I wake up in the morning, I know the day's going to be full and it's
going to demand everything I've got."

The conflict: _____

_____

Formula: _____

_____

_____

Your own words: _____

_____

_____

4. High school teacher, 50, to the principal: "Cindy Smith really got
to me today. She's been a thorn in my side all semester. Just a little
bitch. Asking questions in her 'sweet' way, but everyone knows she's
trying to make an ass of me. Little snot! So I let her have it--I let
it all come out and pasted her up against the wall--verbally, that is.
She was the fool this time. You know me; I just don't do that kind of
thing. I lost control, I have no love for Cindy, but it was a pretty
bad mistake."

The conflict: _____

_____

Formula: _____

_____

_____

Your own words: _____

_____

_____

5. Widowed mother, 47, talking about her son, 17: "He knows he can take
advantage of me. If he stops talking to me or acts sullen for a couple
of days, I go crazy. He gets everything he wants out of me, and I know
it's my own fault. But I still love him very much. After all, he stays
here with me. I do have a man in the house. He's going to be going to
college locally, so he'll be around for a good while yet."

The conflict: _____

_____

Formula: _____

_____

_____

Your own words: _____

_____

_____

EXERCISE 24: The practice of primary-level empathy in everyday life

     If the communication of accurate empathy is to become a part of your
natural communication style, you will have to practice it outside formal
training sessions. That is, it must become part of your everyday
communication style or it will tend to lack genuineness in helping
situations. Practicing empathy "out there" is a relatively simple
process.

1. Bullmer (1975) suggests that empathy is not a normative response in
    everyday conversations. Find this out for yourself. Observe
    everyday conversations. Count how many times in any given
    conversation empathy is used as a response.

2. Next try to observe how often you use empathy as part of your normal style. In the beginning, don't try to increase the number of times you use empathy in day-to-day conversations. Merely observe your usual behavior. What kind of response do you use fairly frequently?

3. Begin to increase the number of times you use accurate empathy. Be as natural as possible. Do not overwhelm others with this response; rather try to incorporate it gradually into your style. You will probably discover that there are quite a few opportunities for using empathy without being phony. Keep some sort of record of how often you use empathy in any given conversation.

4. Observe the impact your use of empathy has on others. Don't set out to use others for the purpose of experimentation, but, as you gradually increase your use of this communication skill naturally, try to see how it influences your conversations. What impact does it have on you? What impact does it have on others?

IV: The Use of Probes in Clarifying Problem Situations

Review the material on probes before doing the exercises in this section. Remember that the purpose of probing is to help the client identify and clarify those experiences, behaviors, and feelings that are relevant to a problem situation or some part of it. Another way of saying this is that a problem is clear if it is spelled out in terms of concrete and specific experiences, behaviors, and feelings that are relevant. Probes are ways of helping clients "fill out the picture," that is, make it more concrete. They are ways of getting at important details that clients do not think of or are reluctant to talk about. An overuse of probes can leave the helper with a great deal of information much of which is irrelevant. When you use a probe, ask yourself: Will this produce the kind of detail which will help the client see the problem situation more clearly, that is, in such a way that he or she might begin to see what he or she might do about it.

EXERCISE 25: Probing for clarity of experiences, behaviors, and feelings

In this exercise a brief problem situation will be presented. You are asked to identify the kind of information in terms of experiences, behaviors, and feelings needed to make the problem clear. These are the things you would probe for if they were not brought up and explored spontaneously by the client. Consider the following example.

Example

A woman, 24, complains that her husband is both psychologically and physically abusive to her. She wonders whether she should get a divorce. What are some of the things that could possibly relate to the clarification of this problem situation?

* What their marriage is like outside times of abuse.
* What good points their marriage has.
* Other defects in their marriage.
* The behavioral form the abuse takes, what he actually does.
* The precipitating factors.
* The pattern of abuse, if any.
* When and where it takes place (public? private?).
* With what frequency.
* How she reacts to the abuse both at the time it is happening and later.
* How she feels about it.
* How long it has been going on.
* How disruptive it is of their marriage.
* How he seems to feel about it.
* How he reacts later.
* Whether he sees it as a problem.
* Whether they discuss the abuse.
* What solutions, if any, have been tried.
* Whether he is willing to seek help.
* Whether he would be willing to come to counseling with her.

In the next two cases make a list of some of the factors--that is, potentially _relevant_ experiences, behaviors, and feelings--that might have to be explored if the problem situation is to be clarified.

1. Grace, 19, an unmarried first-year college student, comes to counseling because of an unexpected and unwanted pregnancy. She believes the father could be either of two young men.
    As in the example above, list some factors that need to be clarified if this young woman is to see the problem situation clearly enough to make informed decisions on handling it.

_____

_____

_____

_____

_____

_____

_____

_____

_____

_____

_____

_____

_____

_____

2. You are a counselor in a halfway house. You are dealing with Tom, 44, who has just been released from prison where he served two years for armed robbery. That was the only offense for which he has ever been convicted. The halfway house experience is designed to help him reintegrate himself into society. Living in the house is voluntary. The immediate problem is that Tom came in drunk last night. Yesterday was supposed to be a job search day for him. Drinking is against the rules of the house.

   List some of the things that need to be clarified if Tom is to see the immediate problem situation clearly enough to make some reasonable decisions.

_____

_____

_____

_____

_____

_____

_____

_____

_____

_____

_____

_____

_____

   Share the probes generated for each case with the members of your training group. Have a discussion as to which probes seem to be the most effective, that is, contribute most to problem clarification.

EXERCISE 26: Combining empathy and probes

In this exercise you are asked first to reply to the client with primary-level accurate empathy and then follow it with a probe. Ask yourself what kind of information or clarification in terms of concrete and specific experiences, behaviors, and/or affect would help the client see the problem situation more clearly. Consider the following examples.

Example 1

Law student, 25, to a school counselor: "I learned yesterday that I've flunked out of school and that there's no recourse. I've seen everybody, but the door is shut tight. What a mess! I have no idea how I'll face my parents. They've paid for my college education and this year of law school. And now I'll have to tell them that it's all down the drain."

Empathy: The whole situation sounds pretty desperate both here and at home. And it sounds so final.

What is needed to make the problem more concrete and clear?   Whom did he actually see and precisely what kind of refusals did he get.

Probe: I'm not sure who you mean by 'everybody' and what doors were shut.

The counselor wants to make sure that the client actually did think of all possibilities.

Example 2

Mental-hospital inpatient, 54, when the topic of moving out of the hospital is brought up in a therapy group: "To tell you the truth, I like it here. So why is everyone here so eager to get me out. Who says that I can't like it here? Is that a crime?"

Empathy: You resent it when people pressure you into thinking of leaving.

What is needed to make the problem more concrete and clear?   It would help to find out what needs are being met in the hospital, what makes it so rewarding for him.

Probe: I'd like to get a clearer picture of some of the things you like about being in the hospital.

First review the different kinds of probes you can use and then respond with both an empathic statement (use the formula or your own words) and a probe to each of the following client statements. Vary the kinds of probes you use.

A caution before doing this exercise. If through your use of empathy clients explore problem situations clearly and concretely, then there is little need for extensive use of probes. Overuse of probes makes clients feel "grilled" and produces useless information. The point here is that even though you are being asked to follow an empathic response with a probe, this in no way means that you should do so automatically in a helping relationship.

1. High school senior to school counselor: "My dad told me the other night that I looked relaxed. Well. I don't feel relaxed. There's a lull right now, because of semester break, but next semester I'm signed up for two math courses, and math really rips me up. But I need it for science since I want to go into pre-med."

Empathy: _____

_____

What needs to be made clearer? _____

_____

Probe: _____

_____

2. Woman, 27, talking to counselor about a relationship that has just ended (she speaks in a rather matter-of-fact voice): "I came back from visiting my parents who live in Nevada and found a letter from Gary. He said that he still loves me but that I'm just not the person for him. In the letter he thanked me for all the good times we had together these last three years. He asked me not to try to contact him because this would only make it more difficult for both of us."

Empathy: _____

_____

What needs to be made clearer? _____

_____

Probe: _____

_____

3. Married man, 25, talking to a counselor about trouble with his mother-in-law: "The way I see it she is really trying to destroy our marriage. She's so conniving. And she's very clever. It's hard to catch her in what she's doing. You know, it's rather subtle. Well, I've

had it! If she's trying to destroy our marriage, she's getting pretty close to achieving her goal."

Empathy: _____

_____

What needs to be made clearer? _____

_____

Probe: _____

_____

4. Woman, 31, talking to an older woman friend: "I just can't stand my job any more! My boss is so unreasonable. He makes all sorts of silly demands on me. The other women in the office are so stuffy, you can't even talk to them. The men are either very blah or after you all the time, you know, on the make. The pay is good, but I don't think it makes up for all the rest. It's been going on like this for almost two years."

Empathy: _____

_____

What needs to be made clearer? _____

_____

Probe: _____

_____

5. Man, 45, talking to a counselor about his use of drugs: "Drugs do mess up my life a bit now and then. I'm not sure that you'd say in any really serious way. At least I know people that are a lot worse off. I'm handling it now. Well, I am more or less handling it. It's no crisis or anything like that."

Empathy: _____

_____

What needs to be made clearer? _____

_____

Probe: _____

_____

6. Divorced woman, 44, talking to a counselor about her drinking; she has just told her "story": "Actually, it's a relief to tell someone. I don't have to give you any excuses or make the story sound right. I

drink because I like to drink; I'm just crazy about the juice, that's all. But I'm under no delusions that telling you is going to solve anything. When I get out of here, I know I'm going straight to a bar and drink. Some new bar, new faces, some place they don't know me."

Empathy: _____

_____

What needs to be made clearer? _____

_____

Probe: _____

_____

7. Man, 57, talking to a counselor about a family problem: "My younger brother--he's 53--has always been a kind of bum. He's always poaching off the rest of the family. Last week my unmarried sister told me that she'd given him some money for a 'business deal.' Business deal, my foot! I'd like to get hold of him and kick his ass! Oh, he's not a vicious guy. Just weak. He's never been able to get a fix on life. But he's got the whole family in turmoil now, and we can't keep going through hell for him."

Empathy: _____

_____

What needs to be made clearer? _____

_____

Probe: _____

_____

8. Woman, 49, talking to a counselor about her relationship with her husband: "To put it frankly, my husband isn't very interested in me sexually any more. We've had sex maybe once or twice in the last two or three months. What makes it worse is that I still have very strong sexual feelings. It seems they're even stronger than they used to be. I keep thinking about this all the time. He doesn't seem very interested at all. I don't know if he's got someone on the side. I'm not handling it well."

Empathy: _____

_____

What needs to be made clearer? _____

_____

Probe: _____

_____

9. Man, 49, talking to a rehabilitation counselor after an operation that has left him with one lung: "I'll never be as active as I used to be. But at least I'm beginning to see that life is still worth living. I have to take a long look at the possibilities, no matter how much they've narrowed. I can't explain it, but there's something good stirring in me."

Empathy: _____

_____

What needs to be made clearer? _____

_____

Probe: _____

_____

10. Woman, 30, talking to a counselor about her dissatisfaction with her life. She is not very talkative: "It's not just life as a whole. I don't seem to care much about myself. (She looks at the floor.) I'm, well, I'm pretty much alone with a person I don't like too much."

Empathy: _____

_____

What needs to be made clearer? _____

_____

Probe: _____

_____

VI. An Overview of Stage I of the Helping Process

The purpose of Stage I is to help clients assess and explore problem situations and clarify them. In Stage II it is essential to help clients develop the kinds of new perspectives needed to set reasonable, problem-managing goals. The following exercises are limited to Stage I.

EXERCISE 27: The identification of common mistakes in Stage I

Here is a list of the some of the mistakes made by helpers as they

assist clients in identifying, exploring, and clarifying problem
situations in Stage I:

* patronizing responses.
* inaccurate empathy.
* advice giving.
* premature use of challenging skills.
* premature pushing of action programs.
* use of cliches.
* judgmental remarks.
* premature or inappropriate use of helper self-sharing.
* inappropriate warmth of sympathy.
* inadequate responses (such as "un-huh" when empathy or a probe might
    be called for or responses that ignore the problem being discussed).
* over use of probes.
* closed, irrelevant, or inappropriate questions.
* condescending responses.
* jargon responses.

   Some of these errors (and perhaps others not mentioned here) are
demonstrated in this exercise. You are asked to sift good from poor
responses.

1. First, if the response seems good to you, that is, if it is
   primary-level accurate empathy or some kind of reasonable probe--give
   it a plus sign (+); however, if it seems to you to be an inadequate
   or a poor response, give it a minus sign (-).

2. Next, indicate the reason or reasons why it seems either good or poor
   to you (use the list of mistakes outlined earlier to help you). Make
   your reasons as specific as possible.

Consider the following example and then proceed to the exercise itself.

Example

Boy, 15, to school counselor: "Mr. Jones [his math teacher] has it in
for me. We haven't gotten along from the start. I don't do anything
different from the other guys, but when there's a blowup, I'm the first
one he blames. I wish he'd get off my back."

Rating

a. (-) "You ought to cool it in his class. Why get thrown out for
something so stupid?"

Reason: advice giving

b. (+) "You feel he's being unfair to you--and that's lousy."

Reason: basic accurate empathy

c. (-) "Jeff, you've been in trouble before. Are you really giving
it to me straight?"

Reason: <u>judgmental, suspicious response</u>

d. (-) "Okay, Jeff. We can straighten this whole thing out if we all just stay calm. By the way, how's the family?"

Reason: <u>placating, patronizing, distracts from problem, nonhelpful</u>

   <u>warmth</u>

e. (+) "You're fed up with the way you see him picking on you. Could you give me a recent example so we could see just what happens?"

Reason: <u>basic empathy plus a reasonable probe</u>

1. Hospital patient, 58, to chaplain: "They've been running these tests on me for three days now. I don't know what's going on. They don't tell me what they're for or what they find, good or bad. The doctor comes in for a moment every now and then, but he doesn't really tell me anything, either. And I still feel so weak and listless."

a. (   ) "Norm, you know these things take time. I'm sure what's happening to you is standard procedure."

Reason: _____

b. (   ) "Is this the first time you've had to go through all of this?"

Reason: _____

c. (   ) "Have your nurse call the doctor and just ask him what's going on. Put a little pressure on him."

Reason: _____

d. (   ) "Well, now, perhaps a little more patience would help everyone, including you."

Reason: _____

e. (   ) "It must be really frustrating being kept in the dark like this. I'm curious as to how you handle this kind of thing outside."

Reason: _____

2. Woman, 22, talking to a job counselor about job interviews: "I wince every time people ask me about my education. As soon as I say 'high school,' I see the lights go out in too many eyes. I feel that I'm as educated as any college grad. I read quite a bit. I deal with people well. I think I've got most of what you're supposed to get from college, except the degree."

a. (   ) "Sure, I see. Well, what do you think you can do?"

Reason: _____

b. (   ) "You feel good about yourself because you've gotten a much better education by doing it yourself."

Reason: _____

c. (   ) "Let's come up with a plan of what to say when they ask you about your education."

Reason: _____

d. (   ) "You resent being categorized when you say 'high school.' You know you're an educated person."

Reason: _____

e. (   ) "You feel rightfully proud about being self-educated. It's something you don't have to apologize for. But I also assume that you're saying that potential employers are going to keep asking you about your formal education."

Reason: _____

3. Man, 32, talking to a counselor about a possible divorce: "I just can't divorce her. My parents would have kittens. They don't really like her, but they believe that marriage is forever. My mother is almost a fanatic about religion. I don't go to church much anymore, myself, but my parents aren't aware of that."

a. (   ) "Maybe it's time to cut the apron strings. Your mother doesn't have to live with your wife. <u>You</u> do."

Reason: _____

b. (   ) "You're pretty nervous about the way your parents are going to react. Could you explain a bit more how their reaction might be influencing your decision?"

Reason: _____

c. (   ) "You feel caught. You don't think your parents would handle it if you were to get a divorce."

Reason: _____

d. (   ) "I got a divorce. My parents didn't like it, but they finally learned how to live with it."

Reason: _____

e. (   ) "I'm not sure whether your wife is also religious."

Reason: _____

4. Woman, 32, who has recently had an abortion talking to a counselor about the impact it has had on her: "I think of the thousands and thousands of women like myself, but right now numbers don't mean a thing. All I have is my reaction and theirs don't count. I wander around the house. I can't get myself to do things. Things between me and Tom [her husband] are very subdued. It's like a conspiracy, we don't talk about it, but it fills our relationship, it fills the house. I don't know whether I'm numb or what."

a. ( ) "What have you done to try to get back into your normal routine.?"

Reason: _____

b. ( ) "You're feeling pretty depressed. That's natural. This is completely different from anything that you've ever done before. So you're going to be feeling some emotions and thinking some thoughts that are new for you. It's a time when you have to trust yourself, trust your decision, trust your relationship to your husband. It's a quiet reflective time for some people. It's an upending time for others."

Reason: _____

c. ( ) "You sound like you're perhaps still somewhat in shock and fairly unsettled. It's not proving easy to come to grips with the fact that you've had an abortion."

Reason: _____

d. ( ) "You haven't been able to make peace with yourself yet. Perhaps you and Tom have to say to each other what it means. This conspiracy of silence with yourself and with him seems to be eating you up."

Reason: _____

e. ( ) "I've come to know you well. You're a strong woman with strong convictions. You wage war, even with yourself, before you make peace. This is the pattern. This is you. It's almost as if your strengths sometimes get the better of you."

Reason: _____

5. High school senior to a school counselor: "As you know, I graduate at the end of the fall semester. I could go right downstate and begin college in the winter semester. That has some advantages. I'd get a kind of head start. And I'd be on my own a little sooner than I expected. But it also means leaving my friends here. I have a sneaking suspicion that the freshmen at the university will all have their circle of friends by now. Maybe I might just stick around here and enjoy doing nothing for a semester."

a. ( ) "It sounds like a kind of toss-up. It would be exciting to get away from home and start college. But you'd hate to end up without friends."

Reason: _____

b. ( ) "It sounds like a fear of loneliness might be a bigger issue for you than you thought."

Reason: _____

c. ( ) "These are the kinds of decisions you seem to handle well. They give you a lot of the character you've got."

Reason: _____

d. ( ) "You're really fortunate. When I was your age, I didn't have the luxury of having that kind of decision to make."

Reason: _____

e. ( ) "Maybe in one sense it's a dilemma for you, Tom, but my bet is that you'd love to be a 'new person on campus.' It's a challenge. I bet you could break into some social circles, no matter how tight knit they would be. Does what I'm saying make any sense to you?"

Reason: _____

6. Resident of a halfway house, 58, talking to activities specialist: "You always hang around with the younger residents, playing pool and listening to that awful music. I don't think you think it's important to be with those of us who are older. I sit in the activities room alone a lot. When you do talk to me, I get the feeling you think you're wasting your time."

a. ( ) "Cathy, you know you're jealous of the younger people. It's a constant theme with you."

Reason: _____

b. ( ) "Come sit with me, Cathy, and we'll work everything out. We'll have a nice chat."

Reason: _____

c. ( ) "If you want to know the real truth, I don't like the young people at all. I have to force myself to be with them. I put on a good act, don't I?"

Reason: _____

d. ( ) "So you think you're not high on my list of priorities. And you resent it."

Reason: _____

e. ( ) "I've got a sneaking suspicion that you've got other things stored up for me, Cathy. Let's have it all out."

Reason: _____

7. Middle-level manager to consultant: "These fools here don't know what they're doing. We're going to end up like the passenger railroads. The union leaders keep pulling the noose tighter and tighter. If a guy even looks at a machine for which he's not 'licensed,' there's an uproar. With the economy the way it is, there just has to be more leeway to move people around. But if you think you can talk sense into the union leaders, you've got another think coming."

a. ( ) "I'm still not sure what the exact point is. Could you elaborate on it a bit."

Reason: _____

b. ( ) "I feel you're attacking _me_, even though I'm not a part of the problem. I'm just a consultant here. I don't run the place."

Reason: _____

c. ( ) "You feel good because at least you've got a handle on what's going wrong."

Reason: _____

d. ( ) "You're saying three things. One, make everyone aware of what impact the economy is having on the business. Two, push for better union leadership. Three, change the licensing law."

Reason: _____

e. ( ) "I can see that you're angry, but I'm not sure where it's getting you."

Reason: _____

EXERCISE 28: Counseling yourself: An exercise in Stage I skills

In this exercise you are asked to carry on a dialogue in writing with yourself.

Choose some problematic area of your life, one that is relevant to your interpersonal style and/ or to your competence as a helper. Use the skills of Stage I to help yourself explore and clarify this area. Stay in Stage I. Do spend time challenging yourself, setting goals, or elaborating action programs. Do use empathy and probing. Study the following example.

Example

This example comes from the experience of a beginning counselor trainee who was working in a halfway house for people who had been in mental institutions. In this dialogue with himself he questions the work he is doing at the house. This is the way he counseled himself.

Self: "I'm not sure I should be working in a halfway house. I've been a psychology major for the last couple of years, but what I've been studying is very theoretical. It doesn't really help me do a better job here. I've got good intentions, but I'm not sure I'm helping anyone."

Response to self: "You just don't feel prepared to do what you're doing. You work hard, but you still feel inadequate."

Self: "I certainly do. I'm pretty much on my own there. I have to figure out what to do. In a sense, I'm trusted, but, since I don't get much supervision, I have to go on my own instincts, and I'm not sure they are always right."

Response to self: "There's some comfort in being trusted, but without supervision you still have a what-am-I-doing-here feeling."

Self: "Sure. There are times when I ask myself just that: 'What are you doing here?' I provide day-to-day services for a lot of people. I listen to them. I take them places, like to the doctor. I get them to participate in conversation or games and things like that. But it seems that I'm always just meeting the needs of the moment. I'm not sure what the long-range goals are and if I--or anyone--am contributing to them in any way."

Response to self: "You get some satisfaction in providing the services you do, but this lack of overall purpose or direction, well that's frustrating."

Self: "Frustrating and depressing. I am depressed. I'm down on myself. Down on the house directors."

Response to self: "You're questioning not just yourself but the whole enterprise."

Self: "That's right. It's a day-to-day operation. In meetings we never talk about the institution. We talk mainly about the patients. We don't talk about philosophy or goals. We talk about incidents! There's got to be some kind of philosophy."

Response to self: "You'd like to see how what you do fits in. It's annoying not to have some kind of mission or philosophy or framework to evaluate what you're doing. You said that there's got to be some kind of philosophy. From what you know, could you spell out what you think the de facto or actual working philosophy or goal is?"

This trainee went on to outline what he saw as the practical philosophy of the halfway house and his dissatisfactions with it. He began to get a much clearer picture of the problem situation.

1. First review this trainee's responses to himself. What kind of responses did he use? How would you evaluate their quality?

2. Now choose a problematic area that is important to you and on separate sheets of paper engage in the same kind of dialogue with yourself. You don't have to start at the beginning of a problem situation. Write a brief description of the problem and then start the dialogue. However, stay within Stage I.

TASK 3: CHALLENGING SKILLS
AND THE DEVELOPMENT OF NEW PERSPECTIVES

Challenging skills include summarizing, information sharing, advanced accurate empathy, confrontation, helper self-sharing, and immediacy. The purpose of these skills is to help clients develop the kind of new perspectives or behavioral insights needed to set problem-managing goals. Therefore, these skills do not represent behaviors that are good in themselves. They are good if they are instrumental, that is, if they help clients complete the process of problem clarification.

I. Summarizing

At a number of points throughout the helping process it is useful for helpers to summarize or to have clients summarize the principal points of their interaction. This has a way of helping clients redirect their energies and it places them under pressure to move on. At this stage of the helping process, this means moving on toward the kind of problem definition and clarification that allows for the setting of behavioral goals. Summarizing can be an effective way of helping a client move from Stage I to Stage II.

EXERCISE 29: Summarizing as an instrument of problem clarification

This exercise assumes that trainees have been using Stage I skills to counsel one another.

1. The total training group is divided into subgroups of three.

2. There are three roles in each subgroup: helper, client, and observer.

3. The helper spends ten minutes counseling the client, using Stage I skills. The client should continue to explore one of the problem areas he or she has chosen to deal with in the training group.

4. At the end of the ten minutes, the helper summarizes the principal points of the interaction. Helpers should try to make the summary both accurate and concise, keeping in mind that it is meant to help the client move toward the kind of problem clarification needed for goal setting. The helper can draw on past interactions if he or she is counseling a "client" that he or she has counseled before.

5. At the end of the summary, the helper should ask the client to draw some sort of implication or conclusion from the summary. That is, the client is asked to take the next step.

6. After this the interaction is stopped and both observer and client give the helper feedback as to the accuracy and the helpfulness of the summary. The helpfulness of the summary is related to the

71

implication or conclusion that the client draws from it.

7. This process is repeated until each person in the subgroup has had an
    opportunity to play each role.

Example 1

It would be too cumbersome to print ten minutes of dialogue here, but
consider this brief outline of a case.

A young man, 22, has been talking about some developmental issues.
One of his concerns is that he sees himself as relating poorly to women.
One side of his face is scarred from a fire two years previous to the
counseling session. He has made some previous remarks about the
difficulties he has relating to women. After ten minutes of interaction,
the helper summarizes:

   Helper: "Dave, let me see if I have the main points you've been
making straight. First, because of the scars, you think you turn
women off before you even get to talk with them. The second point--I
want to check this second point out with you to make sure that this
is what you actually said. Since you come to expect rejection
somewhat automatically, your initial approach to women is cautious,
or cynical, or maybe even subtly hostile."
   Dave: "Yeah, but now that I'm looking at it, I'm not sure that
it's so subtle."
   Helper: "Then the women you meet are cautious with you. Some
might see you as 'mean.' Some steer clear of you because they see
you as a kind of 'difficult person.' What closes the circle is that
you take their caution or aloofness as being turned off by your
physical appearance.
   If these points are fairly accurate, I wonder what implication
you might see in them."
   Dave: "I'm the one that rejects me because of my face.
Nothing's going to be done until I do something about that."

Note that the client draws an implication from the summary ("I am
the primary one who rejects me") and moves on to some minimal declaration
of intent ("I need to change this").

Example 2

A woman, 47, has been talking about her behavior in the training
group. She feels that she is quite nonassertive and that this stands in
the way of being an effective helper. She and her "helper" explore this
theme for about ten minutes and then the helper gives the following
summary:

   Helper: "I'd like to take a moment to pull together the main
points of our conversation. You're convinced that the ability to
'intrude' reasonably into the life of the client is essential for you
as a helper. However, this simply has not been part of your normal
interpersonal style. If anything, you are too hesitant to make
demands on anyone. When you take the role of helper in training
sessions, you feel awkward using empathy and even more awkward using

probes. As a result you let your clients ramble and their problems
remain unfocused. Outside training sessions you still see yourself
as quite passive, except now you're much more aware of it.
      If this is more or less accurate, what implication might you
draw from it?"
      Client: "When I hear it all put together like that, my
immediate reaction is to say that I shouldn't try to be a counselor.
But I think I would be selling myself short."

The feedback should center on the accuracy and the usefulness of the
summary, not on a further exploration of the client's problem. Recall
that feedback is most effective when it is clear, concise, behavioral,
and nonpunitive.

II. Information Giving

As noted in the text, sometimes clients do not get a clear picture of
a problem situation because they are not aware that they lack information
needed for clarity. Information can provide clients with some of the new
perspectives they need to see problem situations as manageable. However,
note that giving clients problem-clarifying information or helping them
find it themselves is not the same as advice giving. Furthermore,
information giving is not to be confused with cliches or amateur
philosophizing.

EXERCISE 30: Information and new perspectives

In this exercise you are asked to consider what kind of information
you might give or help clients get that would help them see the problem
situations they are facing more clearly. Information can, somewhat
artificially, be divided into two kinds: (a) information that helps
them understand their difficulties better, and (b) information about how
they might handle it. In this exercise we are interested in the former.
      Consider the following examples.

Example 1

A young man in his last semester in college came to a counselor
because he was extremely disappointed that he had been unable to get into
graduate school in psychology or counseling. The college he was
attending was the seminary division of a large university. He was a
person of average intellectual ability. He had gotten as far as he had
educationally because he worked extremely hard. He was leaving the
seminary, while most of his friends were staying. A few of his friends
were also leaving the seminary, but they had been accepted in graduate
schools. In his experience, then, most people were going on to some form
of graduate education. He felt that he was a failure and that the world
was shutting him out.

<u>Information for problem clarification</u>. In this case the counselor realized that the client had a number of misconceptions about education and about the relationship between education and successful employment. He shared with the client the educational "pyramid," that is the percentage of people in North America who attend primary school, the percentage that graduate, the percentage who go on to high school, the percentage who graduate, and so on. Once the client saw this "bigger picture," he had a better context in which to deal with his own concern. The counselor shared other information about on-the-job training. Since the client had been in the seminary in both high school and college, he had a very restricted view of the kinds of jobs there were in the world and the kinds of nongraduate training available to prepare for them.

Note that this information sharing session was not a form of advice giving nor was it a subtle way of telling the client that he didn't have a problem. Rather it helped him develop the kinds of new perspectives that would enable him to set his own goals.

In the following cases indicate what kinds of information you believe might help the client see his or her problem situation more clearly. What new perspectives might information provide?

1. A man, 26, has just been sentenced to five years in a penitentiary. He is talking to a chaplain-counselor who has worked at the penitentiary to which the man has been assigned for the past ten years and who had been counseling the man during his trial. The man is deathly afraid of going to prison and has even talked about taking his own life. What kinds of information might help him put his problems in some kind of useful context?

_____

_____

_____

_____

_____

2. A woman, 45, has learned that she has cancer and will soon undergo a mastectomy. She has been put in touch with a self-help group composed of women who have had this operation. She is now talking to one of the members of this group.

_____

_____

_____

_____

_____

3. A woman, 28, has been raped and is talking to a counselor at a rape counseling center. She has not yet reported the rape to the police.

---

4. A man, 34, comes for counseling because he fears he's an alcoholic. He's been drinking heavily for several years and recently has had some physical symptoms that he hasn't experienced before, for instance, blackouts. He has never known anyone who was an alcoholic.

---

5. A man, 41, comes to counseling because he fears he is going crazy. He has a number of problems. His marriage has deteriorated in the past year or so. He and his wife relate poorly to each other. He sees his teenage son and daughter drifting away from him and he doesn't understand this. He is drinking more than he should. He feels depressed, gets out of it, and then feels depressed again. He has begun to steal little things from stores, not because he needs them, but because for some unexplainable reason it gives him a lift.

---

6. Cindy, 23, has been bleeding internally. She is about to undergo a series of tests. She is very frightened and fears the worst. She has never been seriously sick in her life. She fears the doctors, the tests, the hospital. She has never even visited anyone in a hospital.

---

7. Tim, 18, has been smoking marijuana for about three years. He is a fairly heavy user. He has recently received several shocks. His father died suddenly and his steady girlfriend has left him. He has developed fears that he has been doing irreversible genetic damage to himself by smoking pot. He is fearful of giving it up both because he thinks he needs it to carry him over this period of special stress and because he fears withdrawal symptoms.

---

8. Edna, 17, is an unmarried woman who is experiencing her third unexpected and unwanted pregnancy. The other two ended in abortion. She feels guilty about the abortions. She is thinking about keeping this child. For all her promiscuity she seems to know little about sex. She believes that men just take advantage of her.

---

9. Tom, 39, is a businessman who makes frequent trips to Tokyo. He
usually stays at the same hotel and has assumed that he relates very well
with the management. On his present trip he came back to the hotel one
day only to find that his room had been changed. The next week he
returned only to find that he had been assigned a room in a sister hotel
in a nearby part of the city. He is now furious as he relates his story
to Fred, the senior manager of his company in Tokyo. He wants Fred to do
something about it.

_____

_____

_____

_____

_____

10. Maxine, 54, has suffered a stroke which has left her partially
paralyzed on her left side and with speech that is a bit slurred. She is
about to be transferred to a rehabilitation unit. She is depressed.

_____

_____

_____

_____

_____

EXERCISE 31: Information you may need for developing new perspectives
on your own problems

In this exercise you are asked to review the problem areas you have
chosen to deal with during this training program. Choose two areas and
ask yourself whether there is some kind of information that would help
you understand your problem more thoroughly or put it into a better
perspective. Consider the following example.

Example

A trainee, 30, has been married a little over a year. He has just
quit work to start full time in school in a counselor training program.
He is having trouble with his marriage. He is having second thoughts
about quitting his job and entering the program. He has had no

background in psychology previous to this. In college he majored in
history. In doing this exercise, he came up with the following:

    "What kind of information would help me see my problem situation more
clearly?

* I need information about what job opportunities there are for people
like myself with an M.A. in counseling psychology.
* It would be helpful for me (and my wife) to know more about what kinds
of pitfalls exist normatively for a couple in the first two years of
marriage.
* I know vaguely that I'm supposed to be in a particular developmental
period (the age-30 transition) with its own normative crisis. I don't
know anything about that period of life in our culture and how what is
known applies to me.
* I need more feedback on how I am doing in the training program. I am
interested in knowing what my talents in this area seem to be."

    Choose two areas you are working on and ask yourself what kind of
information would help you see yourself and your problem situation more
clearly.

Problem area #1: _____

_____

Information needed: _____

_____

_____

_____

_____

_____

_____

_____

_____

_____

_____

Problem area #2: _____

_____

Information needed: _____

_____

_____

_____

_____

_____

_____

_____

_____

_____

III. Advanced Accurate Empathy

Advanced accurate empathy, described most simply, means sharing hunches about clients and their overt and covert experiences, behaviors, and feelings which you feel will help them see their problems and concerns more clearly and in a context that will enable them to move to goal setting and action. Advanced accurate empathy as hunch sharing can be expressed in a number of ways. Some of these are reviewed briefly below. Before doing the following exercises, however, review the section of advanced empathy in the text.

Some approaches to advanced empathy

* Hunches that help clients see the "bigger picture." Example: "The problem doesn't seem to be just your attitude toward your brother-in-law any more; your resentment seems to have spread somewhat to his fellow workers. Could that be the case?"

* Hunches that help the clients see what they are expressing indirectly or merely implying. Example: "I think I might also be hearing you say that you are more than disappointed--perhaps a bit hurt and maybe even angry."

* Hunches that help clients draw logical conclusions from what they are saying. Example: "From all that you've said about her, it seems that you are also saying that right now you resent having to be with her. I know you haven't said that directly. But I'm wondering if you are feeling that way about her."

* Hunches that help clients open up areas they are only hinting at. Example: "You've brought up sexual matters a number of times, but you

haven't pursued them. My guess is that sex is a pretty important area for you--but perhaps pretty touchy, too."

* Hunches that help clients see things they may be <u>overlooking</u>. Example: "I wonder if it's possible that some people take your wit too personally, that they see it as sarcasm rather than humor."

* Hunches that help clients identify <u>themes</u>. Example: "If I'm not mistaken, you've mentioned in two or three different ways that it is sometimes difficult for you to stick up for your own legitimate rights. For instance . . . ."

* Hunches that help clients <u>own</u> only partially experiences, behaviors, and/or feelings. Example: "You sound as if you have already decided to marry him, but I don't think that I hear you saying that directly."

EXERCISE 32: Tentativeness in the use of challenging skills

As noted in the text, challenges as usually more effective if they do not sound like accusations. Therefore, in delivering challenges such as advanced accurate empathy, it helps to run a middle course between accusing a client and being so tentative that the force of the challenge is lost.

1. In the examples of the different kinds of hunches just outlined, underline the words or phrases that you think add tentativeness to the challenge.

2. Indicate whether you believe that a useful degree of tentativeness has been expressed.

3. List other ways in which you believe that tentativeness can be expressed (that is, other than the ways used in the examples).

EXERCISE 33: Advanced accurate empathy--hunches about oneself

One way to get an experiential feeling for advanced accurate empathy is to explore <u>at two levels</u> some situation or issue in your own life that you would like to understand more clearly. One level of understanding could be called the more subjective level or the more surface level. The second could be called a more objective or a deeper level.

1. Review the material on advanced accurate empathy.
2. Read the examples given below.
3. Choose some issue, topic, situation, or relationship that you have been investigating and which you would like to understand more fully with a view to taking some kind of action on it. As usual choose issues that you are willing to share with the members of your training group and try to choose issues that might affect the quality of your counseling.
4. First, briefly describe the issue, as in the examples.

5. Then give your present "surface-level" or more subjective description of the issue.
6. Next, share some hunch you have about yourself that relates to that issue. Go "below the surface," as it were. Try to develop a new perspective on yourself and that issue, one that might help you see the issue more clearly so that you might begin to think of how you might act on it.
7. In some way suggested by your instructor share your examples with one or more members of your group and give one another feedback.

Example 1: A man, 25, in a counselor training group:

Issue: His experience in the training group is giving him some second thoughts about his ability and willingness to get close to others.

Level 1: "I like people and I show this by my willingness to work hard with them. For instance, in this group I see myself as a hard worker. I listen to others carefully and I try to respond carefully. I see myself as a very active member of this group. I take the initiative in contacting others. I like working with the people here."

Level 2: "If I look closer at what I'm doing here, I realize that underneath my 'hardworking' and competent exterior, I am uncomfortable. I come to these sessions with more misgivings than I have admitted, even to myself. My hunch is that I am fairly fearful of human closeness. I am afraid both here and in a couple of relationships outside the group that someone is going to ask me for more than I want to give. This keeps me on edge here. It keeps me on edge in a couple of relationships outside. There are a couple of members of this group that I am afraid of."

Now this trainee can talk to specific members of the group and discuss what he fears might be asked of him. This is a step toward handling his fear of closeness.

Example 2: A woman, 33, in a counselor training group:

Issue: Her experience in the group is making her explore her attitude toward herself. It might not be as positive as she thought. She sees this as something that could interfere with her effectiveness as counselor.

Level 1: "I like myself. I base this on the fact that I seem to relate freely to others. There are a number of things I like specifically about myself. I'm a hard worker. And I think I can work hard with others as a helper. I'm demanding of myself, but I don't place unreasonable demands on others."

Level 2: "If I look more closely at myself, I see that when I work hard it is because I feel I have to. My hunch is that 'I have to' counts more in my hard work than 'I want to.' I get pleasure out of working hard, but it also keeps me from feeling guilty. If I don't work 'hard enough,' then I can feel guilty or down on myself. I am beginning to feel that there is too much of the 'I must be a perfect person' in me. I judge myself _and_ others more harshly than I care to think."

She goes on to explore the kinds of "sentences" she says to herself about herself and the ways in which she might be judging her fellow trainees.

First, choose four areas, issues, or concerns in your life around which you might develop the kinds of advanced empathic hunches illustrated in the examples. Just choose the areas without spelling out the hunches.

a. _____

_____

b. _____

_____

c. _____

_____

d. _____

_____

As in the examples, develop Level 1 and Level 2 (advanced empathic hunches about yourself--your experiences, your behaviors, your feelings--in each area. Do this on separate sheets of paper.

EXERCISE 34: The distinction between primary-level and advanced accurate empathy

In this exercise, assume that the helper and the client have established a good working relationship, that the client's concerns have been explored from his or her perspective, and that the client needs to be challenged to see the problem situation from some new perspective or frame of reference. First review the material in the text dealing with advanced accurate empathy. Then follow these instructions:

1. In each instance, imagine the client speaking directly to you.

2. In (a) respond to what the client has just said with primary-level accurate empathy. Use the formula or your own words.

3. Next, formulate one or two hunches about this person's experiences, behaviors, or feelings, hunches which, when shared, would help him or her see the problem situation more clearly. Use the material in the _Context_ section and what the client says to formulate your hunches. Ask yourself: "On what _cues_ am I basing this hunch?"

4. Then in (b) respond with some form of advanced accurate empathy, that is, share some hunch that you believe will be useful for him or her. Share it in a way that will not put the client off.

Example

Context: A man, 48, husband and father, is exploring the poor relationships he has with his wife and children. In general he feels that he is the victim, that his family is not treating him right (that is, like many clients, he emphasizes his experience rather than his behavior). He has not yet examined the implications of the ways he behaves toward his family. At this point he is talking about his sense of humor.

Client: "For instance, I get a lot of encouragement for being witty at parties. Almost everyone laughs. I think I provide a lot of entertainment, and others like it. But this is another way I seem to flop at home. When I try to be funny, my wife and kids don't laugh, at least not much. At times they even take my humor wrong and get angry. I actually have to watch my step in my own home."

a. Primary-level accurate empathy: "It's irritating when your own family doesn't seem to appreciate what you see as one of your talents."

A hunch: The family wants a husband and father, not a humorist. (or) His humor, especially at home, is not as harmless as he thinks.

b. Advanced empathy: "I wonder whether their reaction to you could be interpreted differently. For instance, they might not want an entertainer at home, but just a husband and father. You know, just you."

1. Context. A first-year engineering graduate student to counselor has been exploring his disappointment with himself and with his performance in school. He has explored such issues as his dislike for the school and for some of the teachers.

Client: "I just don't have much enthusiasm. My grades are just okay--maybe even a little below par. I know I could do better if I wanted to. I don't know why my disappointment with the school and some of the faculty members can get to me so much. It's not like me. Ever since I can remember--even in primary school, when I didn't have any idea what an engineer was--I've wanted to be an engineer. Theoretically, I should be as happy as a lark because I'm in graduate school, but I'm not."

a. Primary-level empathy: _____

_____

_____

Hunch: _____

_____

_____

b. Advanced empathy: _____

_____

_____

_____

2. Context. This man, 64, took an early retirement from work when he
was 62. He and his wife wanted to take full advantage of the years they
had left. But his wife died a year after he retired. At the urging of
friends he has finally come to a counselor. He has been exploring some
of the problems his retirement has created for him. His two married sons
live with their families in other cities. In the counseling sessions he
has been somewhat repetitiously dealing with the theme of loss.

   Client: "I seldom see the kids. I enjoy them and their families a
lot when they do come. I get along real well with their wives. But now
that my wife is gone . . . (pause) . . . and since I've stopped working .
. . (pause) . . . I seem to just ramble around the house aimlessly, which
is not like me at all. I suppose I should get rid of the house, but it's
filled with a lot of memories--bittersweet memories now. There were a
lot of good years here. The years seem to have slipped by and caught me
unawares."

a. Primary-level empathy: _____

_____

_____

Hunch: _____

_____

_____

b. Advanced empathy: _____

_____

_____

_____

3. Context. A single woman, 33, is talking to a minister about the

quality of her social life. She has a very close friend and she counts on her a great deal. She is exploring the ups and downs of this relationship. In the counseling sessions this woman comes on a bit loud and somewhat aggressive.

Client: "Ruth and I are on again off again with each other lately. When we're on, it's great. We have lunch together, go shopping, all that kind of stuff. But sometimes she seems to click off. You know, she tries to avoid me. But that's not easy to do. I keep after her. She's been pretty elusive for about two weeks now. I don't know why she runs away like this. I know we have our differences. She is quieter and I'm the louder type. But our differences don't ordinarily seem to get in the way."

a. Primary-level empathy _____

_____

_____

Hunch: _____

_____

_____

b. Advanced empathy: _____

_____

_____

_____

4. Context. A man, 40, is talking to a marriage counselor. This is the third time he has come to see the counselor over the past four years. His wife has never come with him. The other times he spent only a session or two with the counselor and then dropped out. In this session he has been talking a great deal about his latest annoyances with his wife.

Client: "I could go on telling you what she does and doesn't do. It's a litany. She really knows how to punish, not only me but others. I don't even know why I keep putting up with it. I want her to come to counseling, but she won't come. So, here I am again, in her place."

a. Primary-level empathy_____

_____

_____

Hunch: _____

_____

_____

b. Advanced empathy: _____

_____

_____

_____

5. <u>Context</u>. A high school senior is talking to a school counselor about college and what kinds of courses she might take there. However, she also mentions, somewhat tentatively, her disappointment in not being chosen as valedictorian of her class. She and almost everyone else had expected her to be chosen.

    <u>Client</u>: "I know that I would have liked to have been the class valedictorian, but I'm not so sure that you are supposed to count on anything like that. They chose Jane. She'll be good. She speaks well and she's very popular. But no one has a <u>right</u> to be valedictorian. I'd be kidding myself if I thought differently. I've done better in school than Jane, but I'm not as outgoing or popular."

a. Primary-level empathy: _____

_____

_____

Hunch: _____

_____

_____

b. Advanced empathy: _____

_____

_____

6. <u>Context</u>. A college professor, 43, is talking to a friend, who happens to be a counselor, about his values. He is vaguely dissatisfied with his priorities, but has never done much about examining his current values in any serious way. From time to time the two of them talk about values, but no conclusions are reached. He is not married. Work seems to be a primary value.

Client: "Well, it's no news to you that I work a lot. There's literally no day I get up and say to myself, 'Well, today is a day off and I can just do what I want.' It sounds terrible when I put it that way. I've been going on like that for about ten years now. It seems that I should do something about it. But it's obviously my choice. I'm doing what I'm doing freely. No one's got a gun to my head."

a. Primary-level empathy:_____

_____

_____

Hunch: _____

_____

_____

b. Advanced empathy: _____

_____

_____

_____

7. Context. A man, 50, with a variety of problems in living is talking with a counselor. His tendency has been to ruminate almost constantly on his defects. He begins a second interview on this somewhat sour note.

Client: "To make myself feel bad, all I have to do is review what has happened to me in the past and take a good look at what is happening to me right now. This past year, I let my drinking problem get the best of me for four months. Over the years, I did lots of things to mess up my marriage. For instance, like changing jobs all the time. Now my wife and I are separated. I don't earn enough money to give her much, and the thought of getting another job is silly with the economy the way it is. I'm not so sure what skills I have to market, anyway."

a. Primary-level empathy: _____

_____

_____

Hunch: _____

_____

_____

b. Advanced empathy: _____

_____

_____

_____

8. <u>Context</u>. A divorced woman, 35, with a daughter, 12, is talking to a
counselor about her current relationships with men. She mentions that she
has lied to her daughter about her sex life. She has told her that she
doesn't have sexual relations with men, but she does.

    <u>Client</u>: "I don't want to hurt my daughter by letting her see my
shadow side. I don't know whether she could handle it. What do you
think? I'd like to be honest and tell her everything. I just don't want
her to think less of me. I like sex. I've been used to it in marriage,
and it's just too hard to give it up. I wish you could tell me what to
do about my daughter."

a. Primary-level empathy: _____

_____

_____

Hunch: _____

_____

_____

b. Advanced empathy: _____

_____

_____

_____

9. <u>Context</u>. The wife of this man, 35, has recently left him. He tried
desperately to get her back, but she wanted a divorce. As part of his
strategy to get her back he examined his role in the marriage and freely
"confessed" to both the counselor and his wife what he felt he was doing
wrong in the relationship. Before that, part of his problem in his
relationship with both his wife and others was a need to get the better
of her and others in arguments. He could never admit that he might have
been wrong.

    <u>Client</u>: "I don't know what's wrong with her. I've given her
everything she wanted. I mean I've admitted all my mistakes. I was even
willing to take the blame for things that I thought were her fault. Now
my hands are tied--damned if you do and damned if you don't."

a. Primary-level empathy: _____

_____

_____

Hunch: _____

_____

_____

b. Advanced empathy: _____

_____

_____

10. A nun, 42, a member of a counselor training group, has been talking about her dissatisfaction with her present job. Although a nurse, she is presently teaching in a primary school because, she says, of the "urgent needs" of that school. When pressed, she refers briefly to a history of job dissatisfaction. In the group she has shown herself to be an intelligent and caring woman, but she tends to speak and act in self-effacing ways.

Sister N.: "The reason I'm talking about my job is that I don't want to become a counselor and then discover it's another job I'm dissatisfied with. It would be unfair to the people I'd be working with and unfair to the religious order that's paying for my education."

a. Primary-level empathy: _____

_____

_____

Hunch: _____

_____

_____

b. Advanced empathy: _____

_____

_____

_____

IV. Helper Self-Disclosure

Although helpers should be <u>ready</u> to make disclosures about themselves
that would help their clients understand their problem situations more
clearly, they should do so only if such disclosures do not upset and
distract their clients from the work they are doing.

EXERCISE 35: Experiences of mine that might be helpful to others

In this exercise you are asked to review some problems in living
which you feel that you have managed or are managing successfully.
Indicate what you might share about yourself that would help a client
with a <u>similar</u> problem situation understand that problem situation or
some part of it more clearly. That is, what might you share of yourself
that would help the client move forward in the problem-managing process?
First consider the following examples.

Example 1

   <u>Trainee</u>: "In the past I have been an expert in feeling sorry for
myself whenever I had to face any kind of problem situation. I know very
well the rewards of seeing myself as victim. I used to phantasize myself
as victim as a form of daydreaming or recreation. I think many clients
get mired down in their problems because they <u>let</u> themselves feel sorry
for themselves the way I did. I think I can spot this tendency in
others. When I see this happening, I think I could share brief examples
from my own experience and then ask clients to see if what I was doing
squares with what they see themselves doing now."

Example 2

   <u>Trainee</u>: "I have been addicted to a number of things in my life and
I see a common pattern in different kinds of addiction. For instance, I
have been addicted to alcohol, to cigarettes, and to sleeping pills. I
have also been addicted to people. By this I mean that at times in my
life I have been a very dependent person and I found the same kind of
symptoms in dependency that I did in addiction. I know a lot about the
fear of letting go and of the pain of withdrawal. I think I could share
some of this in ways that would not accuse or frighten clients or
distract them from their own concerns."

1. List four areas in which you feel you have something to share that
    might help clients who have problems in living similar to your own.
    Just briefly indicate the area.

a. _____

    _____

b. _____

_____

c. _____

_____

d. _____

_____

2. Next, on separate paper make more extended comments in each area, comments similar to those in the examples.

EXERCISE 36: Appropriateness of helper self-disclosure

In this exercise you are asked to review the client situations presented in Exercise 34. In each case, ask yourself whether you feel that sharing your own experience might in some way help the client. Note that this does not mean that you would necessarily share your experience. You are being asked only to see whether you have some experience that might help the client see his or her problem more clearly. Consider the following example (which is the example used in Exercise 34).

Example

Context. A man, 48, husband and father, is exploring the poor relationships he has with his wife and children. In general he feels that he is the victim. He feels that his family is not treating him right, that is, like many clients he emphasizes what others are doing to him rather than his own behavior. He has not yet examined the implications of the ways he behaves toward his family. At this point he is talking about his sense of humor.

Client. "For instance, I get a lot of encouragement for being witty at parties. Almost everyone laughs. I think I provide a lot of entertainment, and others like it. But this is another way I seem to flop at home. When I try to be funny, my wife and kids don't laugh, at least not much. At times they even take my humor wrong and get angry. I actually have to watch my step in my own home."

First of all, assume that you respond with primary-level accurate empathy, as in Exercise 34. Then ask yourself whether you have any experience that might help the client see the problem situation more clearly. If so, then mention what this experience is.

My experience: A person who was trying to become close to me once told me that he found it difficult to get past my humor and make contact with me. I was startled and began to see how I was using humor to keep people at a distance. In my case, it was one way I controlled what happened in relationships.

Now review each case in Exercise 34 and see whether you have some personal experience that might help the client get a better grasp of his or her problem. On separate paper jot down what you think could be helpful if you presented it in the right way.

EXERCISE 37: Practicing self-sharing in counseling interviews

In this exercise, you are asked to try your hand at sharing your experience to help your "client" see his or her problem situation more clearly.

1. The training group should be divided into groups of three--helper, client, and observer.
2. The client should continue to discuss a problem situation with which the helper is familiar, that is, one that has been explored in terms of Stage I.
3. Spend between five and ten minutes in a helping session. If you are the helper, once or twice during the session try to share some experience of yours that you think might help the client. Be brief and focused. Present your experience in such a way as not to distract the client from his or her own concerns.
4. When time is up, the observer and client give the helper feedback on the usefulness of the disclosure.
   * How pertinent was it?
   * Was it brief and focused?
   * Did the helper present it in such a way as to keep the attention on the client's concerns?
   * Did the client make use of the helper's disclosure? Did it help make the problem situation or some part of it clearer?

Consider the following example (related to the example in Exercise 36).

Example

Helper: "I don't use a lot of humor at home, but if I don't watch out, I can talk endlessly about sports. I think my family wants me to talk to them, but I also think they want me to monitor the amount of time I spend in sports talk. I've been wondering whether your wife and kids might have similar feelings about your humor."

Repeat this exercise until each member of the three-person group has had the opportunity to be helper.

V. Confrontation: Dealing with Discrepancies

Confrontation is a skill in which you <u>invite</u> clients to examine discrepancies that they are perhaps overlooking and which keep them locked into problem situations. Review the material on confrontation in the text before doing these exercises. Note especially that confrontations are meant to be <u>instrumental</u>, that is, they are useful to the degree that they help clients develop the kind of new perspectives that serve to define and clarify problem situations. Furthermore, confrontations are meant to be <u>descriptions</u> rather than accusations. If they sound like accusations rather than invitations, they tend to elicit defensive reactions in clients.

EXERCISE 38: Confronting one's own strengths

One of the best forms of confrontation is to invite clients to examine strengths and resources they are not using but which could be used to manage some problem situation more effectively. The discrepancy is that the strength is there but is not being used or used as fully as it might. In this exercise you are asked to confront yourself with respect to your own unused strengths and resources. Consider the following example.

Example

<u>Problem situation</u>. "My social life is not nearly as full as I would like it to be."

<u>Description of unused strengths or resources</u>. "I have problem-solving skills, but I don't apply them to the practical problems of everyday life such as my less than adequate social life. Instead of defining goals for myself (making acquaintances, developing friendships) and then seeing how many different ways I could go about achieving these goals, I 'wait around' to see if something will happen to make my social life fuller. I remain passive even though I have the skills to become active."

Now consider four problem situations or parts of problem situations you have been working on.

1. Briefly identify the problem situation.
2. Describe the problem situation or some part of it in terms of some strength, ability, or resource you are not using or are not using as fully as you might.

1. Problem situation: _____

_____

Unused strength: _____

_____ _____

_____

_____

_____

_____

2. Problem situation: _____

_____

Unused strength: _____

_____

_____

_____

_____

_____

3. Problem situation: _____

_____

Unused strength: _____

_____

_____

_____

_____

_____

4. Problem situation: _____

_____

Unused strength: _____

_____

_____

_____

_____

_____

EXERCISE 39: Further self-confrontation

Most of us face a variety of self-defeating discrepancies in our
lives besides the discrepancies that involve unused strengths and
resources. We all allow ourselves, to a greater or lesser extent, to
become victims of our own prejudices, smokescreens, distortions, and
self-deceptions. In this exercise you are asked to confront some of
these, especially the kind of discrepancies that might affect the quality
of your helping or the quality of your membership in the training group.
Consider the following examples.

Example 1

   The issue. This trainee confronts himself on being controlling in
his relationships with others.

   Trainee: "I am very controlling in my relationships with others.
For instance, in social situations I manipulate people into doing what I
want to do. I do this as subtly as possible. I find out what everyone
wants to do and then I use one against the other and gentle persuasion to
steer people in the direction in which I want to go. In the training
sessions I try to get people to talk about problems that are of interest
to me. I even use empathy and probes to steer people in directions I
might find interesting. All this benign manipulation is so much a part
of my style that usually I don't even notice it. I see this as selfish,
but yet I experience little guilt when I think about it."

Example 2

   The issue. This trainee confronts her need for approval from others.

   Trainee: "Most people see me as a 'nice' person. Part of this I
like, part of it is a smokescreen. Being nice is my best defense against
harshness and criticism from others. I'm cooperative. I compliment
others easily. I'm not cynical or sarcastic. I've gotten to enjoy this
kind of being 'nice.' I find it rewarding. But it also means that I
seldom talk about ideas that might offend others. My feedback to others
in the group is almost always positive. I let others give feedback on
mistakes. Outside the group I steer clear of controversial
conversations. But I'm beginning to feel very bland."

Now confront yourself in three areas that, if dealt with, will help
you be a more effective trainee and helper.

1. The issue. _____

_____

Descriptive self-confrontation: _____

_____

_____

_____

_____

_____

_____

_____

_____

2. The issue. _____

_____

Descriptive self-confrontation: _____

_____

_____

_____

_____

_____

_____

_____

_____

3. The issue. _____

_____

Descriptive self-confrontation: _____

_____

_____

_____

_____

_____

_____

_____

_____

_____

EXERCISE 40: The confrontation round robin: Confronting and responding
   to confrontation

   The purpose of this exercise is to give you the opportunity to
practice both confrontation and nondefensive response to confrontation.
The assumption is that you have begun to know the other members of your
training group fairly well.

1. Review the material on confrontation and effective response to
    confrontation in the text.
2. Choose partners. In a six-person group there will be partners A-B,
    C-D, and E-F. Partners A, C, and E (a) point out something they have
    noticed that their partners do well in the training group and then
    (b) challenge their partners in some way (for instance, by pointing
    out a strength or resource that is being underused).
3. The partners of the challengers, B, D, and F respond first with
    accurate empathy to make sure that they understand the point of the
    challenge.
4. Then the partners proceed to discuss the challenge briefly in terms
    of concrete experiences, behaviors, and feelings.
5. The second partner, B, D, and F then becomes the challenger and the
    process is repeated.
6. If possible, each member of the training group should have an
    opportunity both to challenge and be challenged by every other member
    of the training group.

Example

   Partner A: "In our group sessions, you take pains to see to it that
other members of the group are understood, especially when they talk
about sensitive issues. You provide a great deal of empathy and you
encourage others, principally by your example, to do the same. Your
empathy never sounds phony and most of the time you're quite accurate.
   "However, you tend to limit yourself to primary-level empathy. You
seldom use probes and you seem to be slow to challenge anyone, for
instance, by sharing hunches that would help others see their

interactional styles more clearly. Because of your empathy and genuineness, you have amassed a lot of 'credits' in the group, but you don't use them to help others make reasonable demands on themselves."

B's response: "You appreciate my ability and willingness to be empathic. But I am less effective than I might be in that I don't move beyond primary-level empathy, especially since I 'merit' doing so. I should work on increasing my challenging skills."

A and B then spend <u>a few minutes</u> exploring the issue that has been raised.

VI. Immediacy: Exploring Relationships

As noted in the text, your ability to deal directly with what is happening between you and your clients in the helping sessions themselves is an important skill. <u>Relationship</u> immediacy refers to your ability to review the history and present status of your relationship to another person in concrete behavioral ways. <u>Here-and-now</u> immediacy refers to your ability to deal with a particular situation that is affecting the ways in which you and the other person are relating right now, in this moment.

Immediacy is a complex skill. It involves (1) revealing how you are being affected by the other person, (2) sharing hunches about his or her behavior towards you or pointing out discrepancies, distortions, smokescreens, and the like, and (3) inviting the other person to explore the relationship with a view to developing a better working relationship. For instance, if you see that a client is manifesting hostility towards you in subtle, hard-to-get-at ways, you may: (1) let the client know how you are being affected by what is happening in the relationship (self-disclosure), (2) describe the client's behavior and share reasonable hunches about what is happening (challenge), and (3) invite the client to examine in a direct way what is happening in the relationship. Immediacy involves collaborative problem solving with respect to the relationship itself.

EXERCISE 41: Immediacy in your interpersonal life

In this exercise you are asked to review some issues that remain "unfinished" between you and others outside the training group.

1. Think of people in your life with whom you have some unresolved or undealt-with "you-me" issues (relatives, friends, intimates, coworkers, and so forth).
2. Briefly indicate what the issue is.
3. Imagine yourself talking with one of these individuals face to face.
4. Be immediate with this person with a view to instituting the kind of dialogue that would help the two of you grapple with the issue that concerns you. Your immediacy statement should include (a) self-disclosure on your part (the issue and how it is affecting you), (b) some kind of concrete challenge in the form of advanced empathy

or confrontation, and (c) an invitation to the other to engage in dialogue with you on this issue.

5. The tentativeness that best characterizes initial challenges should be evident in your statement.

Consider the following examples.

Example 1

The issue. A trainee sees herself speaking to a friend outside the group. She is dissatisfied with the depth of sharing in the relationship. She is hesitant about revealing her own deeper thoughts, values, and concerns.

Trainee talking directly to her friend: "I'm a bit embarrassed about what I'm going to say. I think we enjoy being with each other. But I feel some reluctance in talking to you about some of my deeper thoughts and concerns. And, if I'm not mistaken, I see some of the same kind of reluctance in you. For instance, the other day both of us seemed to be pretty awkward when we talked a bit about our feelings about religion. We dropped the subject pretty quickly. I'm embarrassed right now because I feel that I may be violating the 'not-too-deep' rule that we've perhaps stumbled into. I'm wondering what you might think about all this."

Example 2

The issue. A trainee is speaking about her relationship to her boss. She feels that he respects her but, because she is a woman, he does not think of her as a prospect for managerial training.

The trainee talking to her boss: "I think you see me as a good worker. As far as I can tell, you and I work well together. Even though you're my boss, I see a sort of equality between us. I mean that you don't push your boss role. And yet something bothers me. Every now and then I pick up cues that you don't think of me when you're considering people for managerial training slots. You seem to be very satisfied with my work, but part of that seems to be being satisfied with keeping me in the slot I'm in. I don't see you as offensively sexist at all, but something tells me that you might unconsciously think of men for training slots before women. Maybe its part of the culture here. It would be helpful for me if we could explore this a bit."

Now write out three statements of immediacy dealing with people in your life outside the training group. Choose people and issues that you would be willing to discuss in the group.

1. The issue. _____

_____

_____

_____

Write out a face-to-face statement on separate paper.

2. The issue. _____

_____

_____

_____

Write out a face-to-face statement on separate paper.

3. The issue. _____

_____

_____

_____

Write out a face-to-face statement on separate paper.

EXERCISE 42: Responding to situations calling for immediacy

In this exercise a number of situations calling for some kind of
immediacy on your part are described. You are asked to consider each
situation and respond with some statement of immediacy. Consider the
following example.

Example

Situation. This client, a man, 44, engages in a great deal of second
guessing with you. He tells you what he thinks you're thinking and
feeling about him. He suggests goals and programs that he thinks you
would want him to choose and engage in. You have tried to ignore this
behavior, but finally you are letting yourself get angry. He has good
verbal skills and sometimes you feel that you are fighting for "on" time
with him.

Immediacy response: "I'd like to explore what's happening between you
and me in our sessions for a moment. I notice that I'm letting something
bother me and have not talked about it. At times you suggest ways you
think I'm thinking about you and courses of action that you think I want
you to follow. Often enough these are your ideas and not mine. We've
gotten into a couple of arguments over this. You argue well. It's
almost as if we've got a little game going. You second guess. I resent
it and say nothing or let myself get caught in an argument with you. My
bet is that our 'game,' if it can be called that, is not contributing
much to our work here. That's my perception. I'd like to hear your
side."

Now consider the following situations and form an immediacy response.

1. <u>The situation</u>. The client is a person of the opposite sex. You have had several sessions with this person. It has become evident that the person is attracted to you and has begun to make thinly disguised overtures for more intimacy. The person finds you both socially and sexually attractive. Some of the overtures have sexual overtones.

Immediacy response: _____

_____

_____

_____

_____

_____

_____

_____

2. <u>The situation</u>. In the first session you and the client, a relatively successful businessman, 40, have discussed the issue of fees. At that time you mentioned that it is difficult for you to talk about money, but you finally settled on a fee at the modest end of the going rates. He told you that he thought that the fee was "more than fair." However, during the next few sessions he drops hints about how expensive this venture is proving to be. He talks about getting finished as quickly as possible and intimates that that is your responsibility. You, who thought that the money issue had been resolved, find it still very much alive.

Immediacy response: _____

_____

_____

_____

_____

_____

_____

_____

3. <u>The situation</u>. The client is a male, 22, who is obliged to see you as part of being put on probation for a crime he committed. He is cooperative for a session or two and then becomes quite resistant. His resistance takes the form of both subtle and not too subtle questioning of your competence, questioning the value of this kind of helping, and of coming late for sessions, and generally of treating you like an unnecessary burden.

Immediacy response: _____

_____

_____

_____

_____

_____

_____

_____

4. <u>The situation</u>. The client, 19, reminds you of your own daughter, 17, toward whom you have mixed feelings as she struggles to establish some kind of reasonable independence from you. The client at times acts in very dependent ways toward you, telling you that she is glad that you are helping her, asking your advice, and in various ways taking a "little girl" posture toward you. At other times she seems to wish that she didn't have anything to do with you at all and accuses you of being "like her father."

Immediacy response: _____

_____

_____

_____

_____

_____

_____

_____

_____

EXERCISE 43:   Immediacy with the other members of your training group

1. Review the general directions for Exercise 42.
2. Read the example below.
3. On separate paper, write out a statement of immediacy for one of the members of your training group (or selected members if the group is large). Imagine yourself in a face-to-face situation with each member successively. Deal with real issues that pertain to the training sessions, interactional style, and so forth.
4. In a round robin, share with each of the other members of the group the statement you have written for him or her.
5. The person listening to the immediacy statement should reply with accurate empathy, making sure that he or she has heard the statement correctly.
6. Listen to the immediacy statement the other person has for you and then reply with empathy.
7. Finally, discuss for a few minutes the quality of your relationship with each other in the training group.
8. Continue with the round robin until each person has had the opportunity to share an immediacy statement with every other member.

Example

Trainee A to trainee B: "I notice that you and I have relatively little interaction in the group. You give me little feedback; I give you little feedback. It's almost as if there is some kind of conspiracy of non-interaction between us. I like you and the way you act in the group. For instance, I like the way you challenge others, carefully but without any apology. I think I refrain from giving you feedback, at least negative feedback, because I don't want to alienate you. I do little to make contact with you. I have a hunch that you'd like to talk to me more than you do, but it's just a hunch. I'd like to hear your side of our story, or non-story as the case might be."

Point out the elements of immediacy--self-disclosure, challenge, invitation--in this example. Then move on to the exercise.

TASK 4: GOAL SETTING

As we have seen, Steps 1, 2, and 3, of the helping process, including assessment, focusing and initial problem exploration, and developing new perspectives, result in the kind of problem clarification that points toward problem-managing action. Goals play a central part in this process. Everything done in the first three steps paves the way for setting realistic goals in Step 4. Everything that follows in Steps 5, 6, 7, and 8 is done to make sure that goals are implemented. A goal is what a client wants to do or accomplish in order to manage a problem situation or some part of it more effectively. Goals are to be distinguished from programs. Goals deal with what is to be accomplished, while programs deal with how a goal is to be implemented. For instance, if a person wants to stop drinking, this is his or her goal. He or she can accomplish this goal in a number of ways, for instance, by joining Alcoholics Anonymous.

The following exercises assume that you have reviewed the material on goal setting in the text.

EXERCISE 44: Making goals more and more concrete

First, read the following example.

Example

Context. Tom, 42, has been discussing his poor relationship with his wife. She has refused to come to the counseling sessions. Tom has stopped blaming her, has explored his own behavior in concrete ways, has developed a variety of new perspectives on himself as a husband and a father, and now wants to do something about what he has learned.

Without learning the specific issues Tom has discussed, use your imagination to come up with four levels of concreteness in a goal shaping process that might apply to Tom's situation. That is, choose four levels of concreteness (from a mere statement of intent to a concrete and specific goal) that you think someone in Tom's position might choose. Obviously, in an actual counseling situation, you would be helping Tom shape his own goals. This exercise deals with goals (what is to be done), not with programs (how any specific goal is to be accomplished).

Level I: Declaration of intent: "I've got to do something about my marriage."

Level II: General mission statement: "I'd like to improve the quality of the time I spend with my wife at home."

Level III: More specific aim: "I want to have better conversations with my wife."

Level IV: More concrete goal: "I'd like to decrease the number of times our conversations turn into arguments or out-and-out fights."

Note that each level becomes more specific in some way. Now do the same with the following situations. Since you do not know the specific issues the client has been discussing, you will have to use your imagination. The purpose of this exercise is to help you develop the ability to move from vague statements of intent to more concrete and specific goals.

1. Context. Linda W., 68, is dying of cancer. She has been talking to a pastoral counselor about her dying. One of her principal concerns is that her husband does not talk to her about her impending death. She has a variety of feelings about dying that well up from time to time such as fear, resentment, anger, and even peace and resignation. She also has thoughts about life and death that she has never had before and has never shared with anyone.

Level I: Statement of intent: _____

_____

Level II: General mission statement: _____

_____

Level III: More specific aim: _____

_____

Level IV: More concrete goal: _____

_____

_____

2. Context: Troy, 30, has been discussing the stress he has been experiencing during this transitional year of his life. Part of the stress relates to his job. He has been working as an accountant with a large firm for the past five years. He makes a decent salary, but he is more and more dissatisfied with the kind of work he is doing. He finds accounting predictable and boring. He doesn't feel that there's much chance for advancement in this company. Many of his associates are much more ambitious than he is.

Level I: Declaration of intent: _____

_____

Level II: General mission statement: _____

_____

Level III: More specific aim: _____

_____

Level IV: More concrete goal: _____

_____

_____

3. <u>Context</u>. Linda, 32, is married and has two small children. Her husband has left her and she has no idea where he is. She has no relatives in the city and only a few acquaintances. She is talking to a counselor in a local community center about her plight. Since her husband was the breadwinner, she now has no income and no savings on which to draw.

Level I: Statement of intent: _____

_____

Level II: General mission statement: _____

_____

Level III: More specific aim: _____

_____

Level IV: More concrete goal: _____

_____

_____

4. <u>Context</u>. Nancy, 19, unmarried, is facing the problem of an unwanted pregnancy. She has a variety of problems. Her parents are extremely upset with her. Her father won't even talk to her. She lives at home and is attending a local community college. These living arrangements are now unsatisfactory to her. Since, for value reasons, she has decided against an abortion, she does not want to live out the remaining months of pregnancy in an atmosphere of hostility and conflict. She is upset because her education is going to be interrupted and finishing college has always been high on her list of priorities. She is unsure about her finances and resents being financially dependent on her parents.

Level I: Statement of intent: _____

_____

Level II: General mission statement: _____

_____

_____

Level III: More specific aim: _____

_____

Level IV: More concrete goal: _____

_____

_____

5. Context. Julian, 51, has just lost a son, 19, in an automobile accident. He (Julian) was driving with his son when they were struck by a car that veered into them from the other side of the road. Julian, who had his seat belt fastened, escaped with only cuts and bruises. His son was thrown through the windshield and killed instantly. The driver of the other car is still in critical condition and may or may not live. Now, ten days after the accident, Julian is still in psychological shock and plagued with anger, guilt, and grief. He has not gone back to work and has been avoiding relatives and friends because he finds "getting sympathy painful." He is separated from his wife and has refused to see her.

Level I: Statement of intent: _____

_____

Level II: General mission statement: _____

_____

Level III: More specific aim: _____

_____

Level IV: More concrete goal: _____

_____

_____

6. Context. Felicity, 44, finds that her nonassertiveness is causing her problems. She is especially bothered at work. She finds that a number of people in the office feel quite free to interrupt her when she is in the middle of a project. She gets angry with herself because her tendency is to put aside what she is doing and try to meet the needs of the person who has interrupted her. As a result, she at times misses important deadlines associated with the projects on which she is working. She feels that others see her as a "soft touch."

Level I: Statement of intent: _____

_____

Level II: General mission statement: _____

_____

Level III: More specific aim: _____

_____

Level IV: More concrete goal: _____

_____

_____

EXERCISE 45: Checking goals against criteria

   A goal, in order to be fully a goal, must meet the following
standards or criteria:

* It must be an <u>accomplishment</u>, an achievement, rather than a program.
* It must be behaviorally <u>clear and specific</u>.
* It must be <u>measurable or verifiable</u>.
* It must be <u>realistic</u>, that is, within the control of the client,
within his or her resources, and environmentally possible.
* It must be <u>adequate</u>, that is, if accomplished, it should in
substantive way contribute to handling the problem situation or some part
of it.
* It must be in keeping with the <u>values</u> of the client.
* It must be accomplished within a <u>reasonable time frame</u>.

1. Return to the goals you have come up with in each of the cases in
Exercise 44 and see whether each of these criteria is fulfilled for each
goal.

2. If the goal does not meet these standards, restate it so that it does.

Example

   Tom's Level IV concrete goal is: "I'd like to decrease the number of
times our conversations turn into arguments or out-and-out fights."

* "Number of fights <u>decreased</u>" is an accomplishment. A new pattern of
behavior would be <u>in place</u>.
* It is behaviorally <u>clear</u>. Tom can get a picture of himself not
arguing or fighting.
* Since Tom has some idea of how often they fight per day or week, he
can <u>verify</u> whether the number of fights has decreased. It would be
better if he indicated how much of a reduction he was looking for.
* Tom cannot control his wife's behavior but he can control his own. If
it takes two to argue or fight, then Tom, by controlling his own behavior
in a variety of ways, can control not arguing or fighting. The
assumption is that Tom has the self-management skills and the

social-emotional resources to do this.
* It makes sense to suppose that a decrease in the number of arguments or fights will contribute substantially to the betterment of their relationship.
* It has to be assumed that taking the kind of unilateral action necessary to reduce the number of fights is in keeping with Tom's values, that he does not feel that he is merely "giving in."
* Tom does not state a time frame. This needs to be added.

Restated goal: "I'd like to reduce the number of arguments or fights we have from an average of two per day to two per week within the next three weeks."

Now review each of the goals you came up with in Exercise 44, apply the criteria, and restate each goal.

EXERCISE 46: Establishing goals for yourself

In this exercise you are asked to relate the process of Exercise 44 to some of your own concerns or problems.

1. Consider four areas of your life that you are trying to manage more effectively. Choose areas of concern you have been working on during the training sessions.

2. On the assumption that you now have a clear picture of each of these areas--that is, you have explored your concern in terms of concrete and specific experiences, behaviors, and feelings and have developed some new perspectives--develop a goal in each area by moving from some kind of statement of intent to a concrete and specific goal.

3. Once you have established a goal, see whether it fulfills the criteria for a concrete and specific goal. If it does not, rework it until it does. Consider the following example.

Example

Area of concern. Jeff, a trainee in a counseling psychology program, has been concerned that he does not have the kind of assertiveness that he now believes helpers need in order to be effective consultants to their clients. He is specifically concerned about the quality of his participation in the training group. He comes up with the following:

Level I: Declaration of intent: "I need to be more assertive if I expect to be an effective helper."

Level II: General mission statement: "I want to take more initiative in this training group."

Level III: More specific aim: "In our open group sessions when there is relatively little structure, I want to speak up without being asked to do so."

Level IV: More concrete goal: "In the next training session, without being asked to do so, I will respond to what others say with empathy. I will respond at least ten times with primary-level empathy when other members talk about themselves."

     Jeff notes that:

* This goal is an <u>accomplishment</u>, that is, a pattern of assertive responding <u>in place</u>.
* It is <u>clear</u>.
* It is quite easy to <u>verify</u> whether he has accomplished his goal or not. He can get feedback from the other members of the group and the trainer.
* He has the skill of empathy but does not use it often enough. He can summon up the courage needed to use the skill. Therefore, the goal is <u>realistic</u>.
* Responding with empathy with some frequency will help him develop, at least in part, the kind of assertiveness called for in helping. In this sense, his goal is <u>adequate</u>.
* It is in keeping with his <u>values</u> of being a good listener and of taking responsibility for himself as a trainee.
* He believes that he can put this new pattern in place by the end of the next meeting. He sees the <u>time frame</u> as reasonable.

     Now follow the same process, relating it to your own concerns. Try to choose two concerns that relate to the quality of your participation in the training group and two that relate to other areas of your life.

1. Area of concern: _____

_____

_____

Declaration of intent: _____

_____

General mission statement: _____

_____

More specific aim: _____

_____

Concrete goal: _____

_____

_____

2. Area of concern: _____

_____

_____

Declaration of intent: _____

_____

General mission statement: _____

_____

More specific aim: _____

_____

Concrete goal: _____

_____

_____

3. Area of concern: _____

_____

_____

Declaration of intent: _____

_____

General mission statement: _____

_____

More specific aim: _____

_____

_____

Concrete goal: _____

_____

_____

4. Area of concern: _____

_____

Declaration of intent: _____

_____

General mission statement: _____

_____

More specific aim: _____

_____

Concrete goal: _____

_____

_____

EXERCISE 47: Helping others set concrete and specific goals

In this exercise you are asked to act as a helper/consultant to one of the members of your training group.

1. Get a partner from among the members of your training group.

2. Decide which is to be helper and which is to be client.

3. If you are the client, give your partner a summary of some problem situation that you are trying to manage more effectively. Be as concrete and specific as possible in this summary.

4. If you are the helper, after listening to the summary, use a combination of empathy, probes, and challenges to help your partner move from a declaration of intent to a concrete and specific goal with the characteristics outlined earlier (that is, an accomplishment that is clear, verifiable, realistic, adequate, in keeping with his or her values, and set in a reasonable time frame). Do not set the goal for your partner. Rather, use your skills to get your partner to use his or her resources in setting some concrete and specific goal.

5. When you feel you have achieved your objective, stop the process and get feedback from your "client" as to how helpful you have been. If you are the client, give feedback that is short and to the point.

6. After the feedback session, choose new partners, with the helpers becoming clients and the clients helpers. Then repeat steps 1 through 5.

TASK 5: DISCOVERING PROGRAM POSSIBILITIES

Goals refer to <u>what</u> clients would like to do to handle problem situations. Programs refer to <u>how</u> they are to accomplish the goals they set. Review the text on program development before doing the exercises in this section.

EXERCISE 48: Brainstorming for program possibilities

Remember that clients sometimes fail to achieve goals, even realistic goals, because their thinking on <u>how</u> their goals might be achieved is too constricted. Brainstorming is a technique you can use to help clients move beyond overly constricted thinking.
Recall the rules of brainstorming:

* Do not criticize any suggestion you come up with. Suggestions are to be evaluated later.
* Quantity is encouraged. Forget about the quality of suggestions for the time being.
* Piggybacking and combining suggestions to make new ones are both allowed.
* Wild possibilities are also encouraged--"One way I could stop eating and lose weight is to have my mouth sewn up."

Consider the following example.

Example

Ira is a member of a group of people who have been selected as high-risk candidates for a heart attack. Some of his relatives have died relatively early in life from heart attacks; he is overweight; he exercises very little; he is under a great deal of pressure in his job; and he smokes over a pack of cigarettes every day. One of his goals is to stop smoking. He would like to stop smoking within a month. He comes up with the following list of program possibilities.

Brainstorming-- Ways of stopping smoking:

* stop cold turkey
* cut down, one less per day until zero is reached
* look at movies of people with lung cancer
* pray for help from God to quit
* use those progressive filters
* switch to a brand I don't like
* switch to a brand that is very heavy in tars and nicotine, one that
  even I see as too much
* smoke constantly until I can't stand it any more
* let people know that I'm quitting
* put an ad in the paper in which I commit myself to stopping
* send a dollar for each cigarette smoked to a cause I don't believe in,
  for instance, the "other" political party

* get hypnotized; through a variety of post-hypnotic suggestions have
    the craving for smoking lessened
* pair smoking with painful electric shocks
* take a pledge before my minister to stop smoking
* join a professional group for those who want to stop smoking
* visit the hospital and talk to people dying of lung cancer
* if I buy cigarettes and have one or two, throw the rest away as soon
    as I come to my senses
* hire someone to follow me around and make fun of me whenever I have
    a cigarette
* have my hands put in casts so I can't hold a cigarette
* don't allow myself to watch television on the days in which I have
    even one cigarette
* reward myself with a fishing trip once I have not smoked for two weeks
* substitute chewing gum for smoking
* avoid friends who smoke
* don't buy cigarettes and therefore be put in the demeaning position of
    having to borrow them
* have a ceremony in which I ritually burn whatever cigarettes I have and
    commit myself to live without them
* suck on hard candy made with the new sweetener Aspertame instead of
    smoking
* give myself points each time I want to smoke a cigarette and don't;
    when I have saved up a number of points reward myself in some way

   Now do the same with the four goals you devised for yourself in
Exercise 46.

Goal 1: _____

_____

_____

_____

On a separate page, brainstorm ways of achieving this goal. Observe the
brainstorming rules. When you think you have run out of possibilities,
force yourself to think of some wilder possibilities.

Goal 2: _____

_____

_____

_____

Brainstorm ways of achieving this goal. Add wilder possibilities at the
end.

Goal 3: _____

_____

_____

_____

Brainstorm ways of accomplishing this goal. At the end, let your
imagination run wild.

Goal 4: _____

_____

_____

_____

EXERCISE 49: Helping others brainstorm program possibilities

     As a counselor/consultant, you can help others stimulate their
imaginations to come up with creative ways of achieving goals. Use
probes based on questions such as the following:

* Who can help you achieve your goal? What people are resources for you?
* What, that is, what things, what resources both inside yourself and
outside can help you accomplish your goals?
* Where, that is, what places can help you achieve your goal?
* When, that is what times or what kind of timing can help you achieve
your goal? Is one time better than another?

1. Choose a partner from among the members of your training group.

2. Decide which one of you will be helper and which client.

3. The client will briefly summarize a concern or problem and a goal
that he or she has decided on as a way of managing the concern. First
of all, help the client state the goal in such a way that it fulfills all
the criteria for a behavioral goal.

4. Next, give the client five minutes to list as many possible ways of
accomplishing the goal that he or she can think of. Have the client
write these down.

5. Then help the client expand the list. Use probes and challenges
based on the above questions.

6. Encourage the client to follow the rules of brainstorming

* Do not allow him or her to criticize the suggestions produced.
* Encourage your client to expand on the suggestions produced, to piggy-
back, to combine.

* When your client goes dry, encourage him or her to come up with wild
possibilities.
* If the client gets stuck, "prime the pump" with a suggestion of your
own, but then encourage the client to go on.
* Reinforce your client ("that's good"), not for "good" suggestions, but
for sheer quantity.

7. When the trainer signals the end of the session, stop and receive
feedback from your client as to the helpfulness of your probes and
challenges.

8. After a couple of minutes of feedback, change partners. If you were
the helper, choose someone who had been a client.

9. Repeat the process.

TASK 6: CHOOSING BEST-FIT PROGRAMS

Brainstorming and other imaginative techniques help clients gather data for the program-development process, but in and of themselves they are not decision-making techniques. They don't in and of themselves help clients do the two things that are necessary at this next point in the helping process, that is (1) choose program elements and (2) put them together in some workable order.

Choosing Program Elements

If brainstorming is successful, clients are sometimes left with more possibilities than they can handle. They may need help in choosing program elements that will work best for them.

EXERCISE 50: Rating program elements

The program elements or courses of action that have been brainstormed, including the wilder ones that have been "tamed" in one way or another, need to be rated in order to discover which will be most useful.

1. Take one of the lists you produced in Exercise 48.

2. Add any further possibilities that have come to mind since doing the list.

3. Give each possibility a number.

4. Review the following C-R-A-V-E criteria for judging the usefulness or the workability of any given program possibility or course of action.

C - Control: To what degree do I have control over this course of action, including control over the resources needed to engage in it?

R - Relevancy: To what degree will this course of action lead to getting the goal accomplished?

A - Attractiveness: To what degree does this course of action appeal to me?

V - Values: To what degree is this course of action in keeping with my values and moral standards?

E - Environment: To what degree is this course of action free from major obstacles in the environment?

5. Use the grid on the next page to rate the program possibilities or courses of action you have discovered through brainstorming on each of the above criteria. Use a scale of 1-5. If a course of action scores

117

Rating Program Possibilities (Courses of Action)

Possibility	Control, Resources	Relevancy	Appeal	Values	Environment
1.					
2.					
3.					
4.					
5.					
6.					
7.					
8.					
9.					
10.					
11.					
12.					
13.					
14.					
15.					
16.					
17.					
18.					
19.					
20.					
21.					
22.					
23.					
24.					

very low on any given criterion, assign a 1. If a course of action
scores very high on any given criterion, assign a 5. Use the other
numbers for points in between. First consider the following examples.

Example 1

A man who wanted to quit smoking considered the following possibility
on his list: "Cut down gradually, that is, every other day eliminate one
cigarette from the 30 I smoke daily. In two months, I would be free."

C - Control: "This is something that is in my control and I have the
'guts' or resources to do it, though it might become much harder toward
the end. Rating: 4."

R - Relevancy: "It leads inevitably to the elimination of my smoking
habit. Rating: 5."

A - Attractiveness: "I very much like the idea of not having to quit all
at once. Rating: 5."

V - Values: "There is something in me that says that I should be able to
quit cold turkey. That has more 'moral' appeal to me. Gradually cutting
down is for 'weaker' people. Rating: 3.

E - Environment: "No one will notice that I am gradually cutting down.
And I'll have time to take a look at what pitfalls, such as friends who
smoke, lie before me. Rating: 5."

Example 2

A young woman has been having fights with a male friend of hers.
Since he is not the kind of person she wants to marry, her goal is to
establish a relationship with him that is less intimate, for instance,
one without sexual relations. She considers the following possibility:
"I'll call a moratorium on our relationship. I'll tell him that I don't
want to see him for four months. Then we can both reestablish a
different kind of relationship if that's what both of us wants at the
time."

C - Control and resources: "I can stop seeing him. I think I have the
assertiveness to tell him exactly what I want and stick to my decision.
Rating: 5."

R - Relevancy: "Since my goal is moving into a different kind of
relationship with him, stepping back and letting old ties and behaviors
die a bit seems to make a great deal of sense. A moratorium is not the
same as ending a relationship, though it may lead to it. Rating: 5."

A - Appeal: "The thought of not having to think about how to relate to
him for a while and the thought of ending the fighting has tremendous
appeal. I also like the idea of not just ending the relationship.
Rating: 5."

<u>V</u> - <u>Values</u>: "I'm not comfortable with this kind of unilateral decision. On the other hand, I don't value having sexual relations with someone I've ruled out as a possible marriage partner. Rating: 4."

<u>E</u> - <u>Environment</u>: "My friends are going to ask me where David is, why I'm not seeing him. Some are going to question my decision. David may try to see me before the moratorium is up. There are a number of bumps in the environment, but they seem manageable. Rating: 3."

In rating your own program possibilities, you are not asked to make the kind of commentary that appears in the examples. Use the CRAVE grid to rate each course of action. Do not spend a great deal of time making the ratings. If for some reason you have difficulty making a rating or have some second thoughts about the rating you do assign, circle the rating and review it later with one of the other members of your training group.

EXERCISE 51: <u>The Balance Sheet</u>

The Balance Sheet is another tool you can use to evaluate different program possibilities or courses of action. It is especially useful when the problem situation is serious and you are having difficulty rating different program possibilities. Consider the following example.

Example

<u>Background</u>. Rev. Alex M. has gone through several agonizing months reevaluating his vocation to the ministry. He finally decides that he wants to leave the ministry and get a secular job. His decision, though painful in coming, leaves him with a great deal of peace. He now wonders just how to go about this. One possibility, now that he has made his decision, is to leave <u>immediately</u>. However, since this is a serious choice, he wants to look at it from all angles. He uses the decision balance sheet to do so.
The format of the Balance Sheet is on the next page. Alex uses it to examine the possibility of leaving his position at his present church immediately. Here are some of the things he finds:

* <u>Benefits for me</u>: Now that I've made my decision, it will be a relief to get away. I want to get away as quickly as possible.
   * <u>Acceptability</u>: I have a right to think of my personal needs.
   * <u>Nonacceptability</u>: I don't have a job and I have practically no savings. I'd be in financial crisis. Further, this course of action seems somewhat impulsive to me, meeting my own needs to be rid of a burden.
* <u>Benefits for significant others</u>: The associate minister of the parish would finally be out from under the burden of these last months. I have been hard to live with.

. . . .

* <u>Costs to significant social settings</u>: Many of the best programs are not rooted in the church system but in me. If I leave immediately, many

The Balance Sheet

The goal: _____

The program possibility or course of action in question: _____

The benefits from taking this course of action:

* For me: _____

    * The acceptability of these benefits: _____

    * Ways in which these gains are not acceptable: _____

* For significant others: _____

    * The acceptability of these benefits: _____

    * Ways in which these gains are not acceptable: _____

* For significant social settings: _____

    * The acceptability of these benefits: _____

    * Ways in which these gains are not acceptable: _____

The losses or costs from taking this course of action:

* For me: _____

    * The acceptability of these losses or costs: _____

    * Ways in which these costs are not acceptable: _____

* For significant others: _____

    * The acceptability of these losses or costs: _____

    * Ways in which these costs are not acceptable: _____

* For significant social settings: _____

    * The acceptability of these losses or costs: _____

    * Ways in which these costs are not acceptable: _____

My overall estimation of this particular program possibility or course of

action _____

of these programs will falter and perhaps die because I have failed to
develop leaders from among the members of the congregation. There will
be no transition period. The congregation can't count on the associate
minister taking over, since he and I have not worked that closely on any
of the programs in question.

> * Acceptability of these costs: The members of the congregation
> need to become more self-sufficient. They should work for what
> they get instead of counting so heavily on their ministers.

> * Unacceptability of these costs: Since I have not worked at
> developing lay leaders, I feel some responsibility for doing some-
> thing to see to it that the programs do not die. Some of my deeper
> feelings say that it isn't fair to pick up and run.

Note that this is just a sampling of parts of the balance sheet the
minister filled out. You are now asked to fill out the entire balance
sheet. Follow these directions:

1. Choose a problem situation which you have clarified and for which you
have established a goal that meets the criteria for a workable goal.

2. Choose a goal for which you have brainstormed program possibilities.

3. Choose a major program possibility or a course of action you would
like to explore much more fully.

4. Identify the "significant others" and the "significant social
settings" that would be affected by your choice.

5. Explore the possible course of action by using the full balance sheet
outlined on the previous page.

Note that the problem area, the goal, and the course of action in
question should have some substance to them. Using the balance sheet to
make a relatively inconsequential choice is not cost efficient.

Note also that the balance sheet can be used to help you make the
kinds of ratings called for in Exercise 50, especially if the course of
action is serious and you're not sure how to rate it.

Putting Program Steps in Order

Many goals call for programs that involve more than one simple step.
If there are a number of steps in a program, then it is important to put
them in some kind of order. What needs to be done first? What needs to
be done second? How many steps are there? These are the kinds of
questions that are asked in putting the steps of a program in the most
workable and cost-efficient sequence. Another way of saying this is that
to achieve certain goals, it may be first necessary to achieve certain
subgoals.

EXERCISE 52: Setting subgoals in the program-development process

   Subgoals are the major steps leading to the accomplishment of a
goal. Consider the following example.

Example

   Eliza, 38, a widow with two children in their upper teens, wants to
get a job. In accomplishment terms, "job obtained and started" is her
goal. However, in talking to a counselor, she soon realizes that there
are a number of steps in a program leading to the accomplishment of this
goal. She comes up with the following major steps or subgoals. She puts
these subgoals in "accomplishment" language, that is, in terms of the
accomplishment to be achieved by the end of each step.

* Step 1: Job criteria established. She soon discovers that she
doesn't want just any kind of job. She has certain standards she would
like to meet insofar as this is possible in the current job market.

* Step 2: Job possibilities canvassed. She needs to find out just what
kinds of jobs that meet her general standards in some way are available.

* Step 3: A "best possibilities" list drawn up. She needs to draw up a
list of possibilities that seem most promising in view of the job market
and the standards she has worked out.

* Step 4: Job interviews applied for and engaged in. She has to find
out whether she wants a particular job and whether the employer wants her.

* Step 5: Best offer chosen and job started. If she receives two or
more offers that meet her standards, she must decide which offer to
accept.

* Contingency plan. If the kind of job search she designs proves
fruitless, she needs to know what she is to do next. She needs a backup
plan.

2. Next, follow this same process in arranging a multi-step program to
achieve one of your own goals.

   a. State a goal you would like to accomplish in order to handle some
concern or problem situation. For instance, choose one of the goals you
set in Exercise 46.

   b. Review the program possibilities (course of action) you
discovered during the brainstorming and scenario writing exercises.

   c. As in the example, indicate one or more subgoals that must be
accomplished if you are to achieve the major goal.

   d. Review each subgoal with one of the members of your training
group. Check to see whether each subgoal has the characteristics
necessary for any kind of goal:

* Is it an <u>accomplishment</u> in its own right?
* Is it <u>clear</u> and specific?
* Is it <u>verifiable</u>, that is, will you know that you have accomplished it?
* Is it <u>realistic</u>, that is, is it something <u>you</u> have to do and something for which you have the resources?
* Is it <u>adequate</u>, that is, is it a major step toward accomplishing the principal goal?
* Is it in keeping with your <u>values</u>?
* Have you established a reasonable <u>time frame</u> for achieving this subgoal?

a. Goal to be accomplished: _____

_____

_____

_____

_____

b. Now indicate the major steps or subgoals that are to be accomplished in moving toward the accomplishment of the major goal.

Subgoal #1: _____

_____

_____

Subgoal # 2: _____

_____

_____

Subgoal #3: _____

_____

_____

Subgoal #4: _____

_____

_____

Subgoal #5: _____

_____

_____

EXERCISE 53: Formulating subprograms

     Just as programs need to be formulated to achieve goals, so
subprograms need to be formulated to reach subgoals. The brainstorming
process in Exercise 48 produces many different program possibilities. One
way of making sense of all these possibilities is to see certain
possibilities as subgoals, that is, major steps on the way to the
principal goal, and other possibilities as subprograms, step-by-step
processes to achieve subgoals.
     Here you are asked to pretend that you are the person in Exercise 52
who is looking for a job. If you were the one looking for a job, how
would you go about accomplishing each of these subgoals?

a. Job criteria established. How would you go about the task of laying
out the standards you would like to see a job meet?

_____

_____

_____

_____

_____

b. Job possibilities canvassed. How would you go about finding out what
kinds of jobs are available?

_____

_____

_____

_____

_____

c. A "best possibilities" list draw up. If your job canvass reveals that
there are a fairly long list of possibilities, what would you do to draw
up a list of the best possibilities?

_____

_____

_____

_____

_____

d. <u>Job interviews applied for and engaged in</u>. How would you go about applying for interviews and what would you want to do in the interviews themselves?

_____

_____

_____

_____

_____

e. <u>Best offer chosen and job started</u>. If you received more than one offer, how would you go about choosing?

_____

_____

_____

_____

_____

EXERCISE 54: Formulating subprograms for yourself

In this exercise you are asked to come up with ways of achieving each subgoal you set for yourself in Exercise 52.

1. Restate your principal goal: _____

_____

_____

_____

2. Now briefly restate each subgoal or major step toward the principal goal together with a brief summary of what subprogram you intend to use to achieve the subgoal. Space is provided for five subgoals. Obviously, your program may have more or fewer subgoals.

Subgoal #1: _____

_____

Summary of subprogram #1: _____

_____

_____

_____

_____

Subgoal #2: _____

_____

Summary of subprogram #2: _____

_____

_____

_____

_____

Subgoal #3: _____

_____

Summary of subprogram #3: _____

_____

_____

_____

_____

Subgoal #4: _____

_____

Summary of subprogram #4 _____

_____

_____

_____

_____

Subgoal #5: _____

_____

Summary of subprogram #5: _____

_____

_____

_____

_____

EXERCISE 55: Developing the resources needed to implement programs

     Counselors can help clients to develop the resources they need to engage in programs that lead to either goals or subgoals. It is a mistake for clients to try programs for which they do not have the resources. In this exercise you are asked to design subprograms that will help clients achieve the subgoal of developing the kinds of resources they need to pursue their principal goals.

1. Mildred and Tom are having trouble with their marriage. They do not handle decisions about finances and about sexual behavior well. Fights dealing with these two areas are frequent. They both agree that their marriage would be better off without these fights and they realized that collaborative decision making with respect to sex and finances would be an ideal.

a. What kind of resources do you think they need to involve themselves in collaborative decision making with each other?

_____

_____

Summarize a program that might help them develop these resources.

_____

_____

_____

_____

_____

b. What kind of resources do you think they need to make better decisions about money?

_____

_____

Summarize a program that might help them develop these resources.

_____

_____

_____

_____

_____

2. Todd feels bad about his impoverished social life. He is now in his
upper twenties and has no intimate female friend and no close friends of
either sex. He feels lonely a great deal of the time. Some of the goals
he sets for himself involve joining social groups, developing wider
circles of acquaintances, and establishing some close friendships.

a. What kind of resources do you think he needs to develop in order to
join and remain in some kind of social group?

_____

_____

Summarize a program that might help him develop these resources.

_____

_____

_____

_____

b. What are some resources you think he probably lacks but will need to
establish some closer and even intimate friendships?

_____

_____

Summarize a program that might help him develop some of these resources.

_____

_____

_____

_____

3. Ruth Ann wants to start a food cooperative in her economically disadvantaged neighborhood in a large city. She gets together a small group of intelligent and interested people. They realize that many such ventures fail. You are a consultant to their undertaking.

What are some of the resources they need to develop in order to move into the work of establishing a cooperative?

_____

_____

Summarize a program that might help them develop some of these resources.

_____

_____

_____

_____

_____

EXERCISE 56: Developing your own resources

In this exercise you are asked to review some of the goals you have established for yourself (for instance, the goals in Exercise 46) and the programs you have been formulating to implement these goals with a view to asking yourself: What kind of resources do I need to develop to engage in these programs? Logistics is the art of having resources ready when they are needed. Resource development, then, becomes a subgoal in the total process and calls for a subprogram. For instance, you may lack the kinds of skills needed to implement a program. If this is a case, then "requisite skills developed or improved" becomes the goal of a resource-development subprogram.

1. Indicate a goal you would like to implement in order to manage some concern or problem situation in some way.

Example

Mark has headaches that disrupt his life. "Frequency of headaches reduced" is one of his goals. "The severity of headaches reduced" is another.

2. Indicate the elements of the program to achieve this goal that call for resources you do not have or do not have as fully as you would like.

131

Example

Being able to relax both physically and psychologically at times of stress and especially when he feels the "aura" that indicates a headache is on its way is part of Mark's program.

3. Point out the resources that you need to develop.

Example

Mark needs the skills associated with relaxing. He also could benefit from learning how to increase alpha waves, the brain waves associated with relaxation, at times of stress. He does not possess either set of skills. Furthermore, since he allows himself to become the victim of stressful thoughts, he also needs some kind of thought-control skills.

4. Summarize a subprogram that would enable you to develop some of these resources.

Example

Mark enrolls in two programs. In one he learns the skills of systematic relaxation and skills related to controlling self-defeating thoughts. In the other, a biofeedback program, he learns how to increase and maintain a high level of alpha waves, especially at times of stress. Fortified with these skills, he is now ready to apply them to a headache-reduction program.

Problem situation #1

a. Your goal: _____

_____

_____

b. Indicate the part of the program that calls for skills or other resources you do not presently have.

_____

_____

_____

c. Indicate concretely and specifically the skills or other resources you would like to develop. Since resource development is a subgoal, what you write should have the characteristics of a workable goal.

_____

_____

_____

_____

_____

d. Summarize a program that can help you develop the resources you need.

_____

_____

_____

_____

Problem situation #2

a. Your goal: _____

_____

_____

b. Indicate the part of the program that calls for skills or other resources you do not presently have.

_____

_____

_____

c. Indicate concretely and specifically the skills or other resources you would like to develop. Since resource development is a subgoal, what you write should have the characteristics of a workable goal.

_____

_____

_____

_____

_____

d. Summarize a program that can help you develop the resources you need.

_____

TASK 7: ACTION
IMPLEMENTING PROGRAMS

Tasks 1, 2, and 3 relate to the definition and clarification of the problem situation. Tasks 4, 5, and 6 relate to devising a <u>strategy</u> for handling the problem situation or some part of it. Task 7 relates to the implementation of the plan or program or strategy. In this task, <u>tactics</u> is the focus. <u>Webster's Seventh New Collegiate Dictionary</u> defines tactics in its military sense as "the science and art of disposing and maneuvering forces in combat." It is not a bad definition since at times the work of implementing programs resembles combat. However, tactics is also defined as "the art or skill of employing available means to accomplish an end [goal]." When clients are "out in the field," as it were, they are more likely to implement programs (strategy) if they can adapt themselves and their programs to changing conditions. <u>Logistics</u>, as we have seen, is the art of having resources available when they are needed. Some of these resources can be developed by clients before they go out "into the field." However, they are more likely to implement programs if they also have the ability to round up resources on the spot.

EXERCISE 57: Force-field analysis--identifying facilitating and restraining forces in program implementation

In this exercise you are asked to identify forces "in the field" that might help you or clients to implement programs and forces that might keep you or clients from implementing programs. The former are called "facilitating forces" and the latter "restraining forces." The use of force-field analysis to prepare yourself is an application of the adage "forewarned is forearmed."

1. Review a goal or immediate subgoal and the program or subprogram (strategy) you have formulated to accomplish it.

2. Picture yourself "in the field" actually trying to implement the program or subprogram.

3. Identify the principal forces that are helping you reach your goal or subgoal.

4. Identify the principal forces that are hindering you from reaching your goal or subgoal.

Example

Marty wants to stop smoking. She has formulated a step-by-step program for doing so. As she is about to begin the program she uses force-field analysis to identify facilitating and restraining forces in the field.

Some of the facilitating forces identified by Marty:

* my own pride
* the satisfaction of knowing I'm keeping a promise I've made to myself
* the excitement of a new program, the very "newness" of it
* the support and encouragement of my husband and my children
* the support of two close friends who are also quitting
* the good feeling of having that "gunk" out of my system
* the money saved and put aside for more reasonable pleasures
* the ability to jog without feeling I'm going to die

Some of the restraining forces identified by Marty:

* the craving to smoke that I take with me everywhere
* seeing other people smoke
* danger times: when I get nervous, after meals, when I feel depressed and discouraged, when I sit and read the paper, when I have a cup of coffee, at night watching television
* being offered cigarettes by friends
* when the novelty of the program wears off (and that could be fairly soon)
* increased appetite for food and the possibility of putting on weight
* my tendency to rationalize things I want to do
* the fact that I've tried to stop smoking several times before and have never succeeded

Now do the same for two goals or subgoals you would like to accomplish.

Situation #1

a. A goal or subgoal you want to accomplish:

_____

_____

_____

b. Picture yourself in the process of implementing the program or subprogram formulated to achieve the goal.

c. List the facilitating forces you see "out there" that are helping or could help you to carry out the program:

_____

_____

_____

_____

_____

_____

_____

_____

_____

_____

d. List the restraining forces at work hindering you from carrying out the program:

_____

_____

_____

_____

_____

_____

_____

_____

_____

_____

Situation #2

a. A goal or subgoal you want to accomplish.

_____

_____

_____

b. Picture yourself in the process of implementing a program or subprogram to accomplish your goal.

c. List the facilitating forces you see that are helping or could help you to implement the program.

_____

_____

_____

_____

_____

_____

_____

_____

_____

d. List the restraining forces that you see hindering you or which might hinder you from implementing the program.

_____

_____

_____

_____

_____

_____

_____

_____

_____

_____

EXERCISE 58: Bolstering facilitating forces

Once you have identified the principal facilitating and restraining forces, you can determine how to bolster critical facilitating forces and neutralize critical restraining forces. In this exercise you are asked to devise ways of bolstering critical facilitating forces.

1. Identify facilitating forces (a) which you see as capable of making a difference in the implementation of a program and (b) which you believe you have the resources to strengthen.

2. Formulate a program for strengthening one or more critical facilitating forces. Choose facilitating forces that have a high

probability of making a difference in the field.

Example

    Klaus is an alcoholic who wants to stop drinking. He joins
Alcoholics Anonymous. During a meeting he is given the names and
telephone numbers of two people whom he is told he may call at any time
of the day or night if he feels he needs help. He sees this as a
critical facilitating force--just knowing that help is around the corner
when he needs it.
    He wants to strengthen this facilitating force.
* First of all, since he sees being able to get help anytime as a kind
of dependency, he talks out the negative feelings he has about being
dependent in this way. In talking, he soon realizes that it is a
temporary form of dependency and that it is <u>instrumental</u> in achieving an
important goal, developing a pattern of sobriety.
* Second, he calls the numbers a couple of times when he is not in
trouble just to get the feel of doing so.
* He puts the numbers in his wallet, he memorizes them, and he puts them
on a piece a paper and carries them in a medical bracelet which tells
people who might find him drunk that he is an alcoholic trying to
overcome his problem.
* He calls the numbers a couple of times when the craving for alcohol is
high and his spirits are low. That is, he gets used to it as a temporary
resource.

<u>Situation #1</u>

a. Briefly describe one or two key facilitating forces from Situation #1
in Exercise 57 that you would like to strengthen.

_____

_____

_____

_____

b. Indicate how you would like to go about strengthening these key
facilitating forces.

_____

_____

_____

_____

_____

_____

Situation #2

a. Briefly indicate one or two key facilitating forces from Situation #2 in Exercise 57 that you would like to strengthen.

_____

_____

_____

_____

b. Briefly indicate how you would like to go about strengthening these key facilitating forces.

_____

_____

_____

_____

_____

EXERCISE 59: Neutralizing or reducing the strength of restraining forces

Sometimes, though not always, it is helpful to try to neutralize or reduce the strength of critical restraining forces.

1. Identify critical restraining forces from your list in Exercise 57, that is, restraining forces (a) which, if neutralized or reduced, would make a significant difference in the implementation of a program and (b) which you feel you have the resources to neutralize or reduce.

2. Formulate a program for neutralizing or reducing these restraining forces.

Example

Ingrid is on welfare, but she has a goal of getting a job. Part of her program is to apply for and go to job interviews. However, she ends up missing a number of the interviews. By examining her behavior, she learns that there are at least two critical restraining forces. One is that she has a poor self-image; she thinks she looks ugly and that the interviewer won't give her a fair chance simply because of her looks. Another is that at the last moment she thinks of a number of "important" tasks that must be done--for instance, visiting her ailing mother--before she can do anything else. She does these tasks instead of going to the interview.

How might Ingrid handle the problem of feeling ashamed of her looks?

_____

_____

_____

_____

_____

How might Ingrid handle the problem of putting "important" tasks ahead of going to job interviews?

_____

_____

_____

_____

_____

Situation #1

a. Briefly indicate one or two critical restraining forces that you identified in Exercise 57 and which you see as critical.

_____

_____

_____

_____

b. What might you do to neutralize or reduce these restraining forces?

_____

_____

_____

_____

_____

Situation #2

a. Briefly indicate one or two key restraining forces that you identified in Exercise 62 and which you see as critical.

_____

_____

_____

_____

b. What might you be able to do to neutralize or reduce these restraining forces?

_____

_____

_____

_____

EXERCISE 60: Identifying obstacles to program implementation--telling your program implementation "story"

As we have suggested in an earlier exercise, "forewarned is forearmed" in the implementation of any given program or subprogram. One way of identifying potential pitfalls is the force-field analysis method seen in previous exercises. Another way is to tell yourself the "story" of what you will encounter as you implement a program.

1. Either with yourself or with one of the members of your training group, begin telling the story of what your effort at implementing some program or subprogram will look like.

2. As you tell the story, jot down the pitfalls or snags you see yourself encountering along the way.

3. Design some kind of subprogram to handle any significant snag or pitfall you see yourself encountering.

Example

Justin has a supervisor at work who, he feels, does not like him. He says that she gives him the worst jobs, asks him to put in overtime when he would rather go home, and talks to him in demeaning ways. In the problem exploration phase of counseling, he discovered that he probably reinforces this tendency in her by buckling under, by giving signs that he feels hurt but helpless, and by failing to challenge her in any direct way. He feels so miserable at work that he wants to do something about it. One option is to move to a different department, but to do so he must have the recommendation of his immediate supervisor. Another possibility is to quit and get a job elsewhere, but the present state of

the economy makes that possibility remote. A third option is to deal
with his supervisor more directly. He sets goals related to this third
option.

One goal is to seek out an interview with his supervisor and tell her
in a strong but nonpunitive way his side of the story and how he feels
about it. The counselor asks him to begin spelling out the "story" of
his implementation of the program to achieve that goal. Some of the
things he says are:

* "I see myself asking her for an appointment. I see myself hesitating
to do so because she might answer me in a sarcastic way. Also, others are
usually around and she might embarrass me and they will want to know
what's going on, why I want to see her, and all that. . . ."

* "I see myself sitting in her office. Instead of being firm and
straightforward, I'm tongue-tied and apologetic. I forget some of the
key points I want to make. I let her brush off some of my complaints and
in general let her control the interaction. . . ."

How can he prepare himself to handle the obstacles or snags he sees in
his first statement? Then what could he do in the situation itself?

_____

_____

_____

_____

_____

How can he prepare himself to handle the pitfalls mentioned in his second
statement? What could he do in the situation itself?

_____

_____

_____

_____

_____

Situation #1

a. Consider some program you want to implement.

b. Begin seeing yourself doing whatever is necessary to implement the
program. Jot down whatever snags or pitfalls you encounter.

Obstacles: _____

_____

_____

_____

_____

c. Indicate how you might <u>prepare</u> yourself to handle a significant obstacle or pitfall and what you might do <u>in the situation itself</u> to handle it.

_____

_____

_____

_____

_____

_____

Situation #2

a. Consider another program you want to implement.

b. In your mind's eye see yourself moving through the program. What obstacles or snags do you encounter? Jot them down.

Obstacles: _____

_____

_____

_____

c. Indicate how you might <u>prepare</u> yourself to handle a significant obstacle you uncover and what you might do <u>in the situation itself</u> to handle it.

_____

_____

_____

_____

_____

_____

EXERCISE 61: The principles of behavior: Learning from program failures

In your text, review the principles of behavior as they apply to the implementation of programs. It seems that many programs flounder and fail because people ignore or misuse such principles and procedures as reinforcement, extinction, punishment, shaping, and avoidance. In this exercise you are asked to review some program failures. You are asked to analyze these failures in terms of these principles of behavior.

* Reinforcement. Were there sufficient rewards or incentives for engaging in the program itself and in each of the steps of the program?
  Example: Corina wanted to graduate from college, but she never learned how to find rewards in studying. Each time she sat down with a text or a written assignment, she was in agony. Sheer "will power" got her through one and a half years of college. But it became too much for her and she quit.

What might she have done? _____

_____

_____

_____

* Punishment. Was punishment misused as a motivator?
  Example: Perry was trying to lose weight. Whenever he ate more that his diet called for he punished himself by calling off some social engagement he enjoyed. This disrupted his social life, punished his friends, and made him feel isolated. When he felt isolated, he tended to compensate by eating.

What might he have done? _____

_____

_____

* Extinction. Were the effects of extinction ignored?
  Example: Lily wanted to read more serious books than her usual paperback novels. She realized that at first she would probably not find that kind of reading as rewarding (exciting) as she found pulp novels. She neither rewarded herself when she did read a serious book nor did she punish herself when she failed to read a serious book that she had intended to read. At the end of a year she found she had read only one serious book and part of a second.

What might she have done? _____

_____

_____

_____

* <u>Shaping</u>. Was the program poorly shaped in terms of sheer amount to be done and in terms of the size of the steps of the program?
   <u>Example</u>: Till's doctor told him that he was prime material for a coronary. He was overweight, he smoked heavily, he drank too much, he did not exercise, and he did not manage the stress of his job or homelife well. Till was scared by what the doctor said. He stopped smoking, he went on a crash diet. He started a rather vigorous exercise program. He became rather bland at work and at home. And he became very depressed and in a few weeks went back to his old style of living.

What might he have done? _____

_____

_____

_____

* <u>Avoidance</u>. Were there more rewards for not engaging in the program or any part of it than for engaging in the program?
   <u>Example</u>: Gretchen and her husband, Al, said that they wanted to talk out problems between them as they came up instead of saving up negative feelings until they burst forth in a game of "uproar." However, whenever one of them did something that annoyed the other, "letting it go this time" seemed more rewarding, or at least less painful, than talking it out. They continued to have their periodic outbursts.

What might they have done? _____

_____

_____

_____

<u>EXERCISE 62: Using the principles of behavior to bolster your
   participation in programs</u>

   In this exercise you are asked to use the principles of behavior to bolster programs you are currently engaged in or are about to undertake.

<u>Situation #1</u>

Briefly describe the goal or subgoal you are trying to achieve and the principal elements of the program you have formulated to reach your goal.

_____

_____

_____

_____

a. How can you use the principle of <u>reinforcement</u> to raise the probability of your engaging effectively in the program? What kinds of <u>incentives</u> will keep you working at the program?

_____

_____

_____

b. How can you apply what you know about <u>punishment</u>, that is, facilitating self-punishment, in a way that will raise the probability of your carrying our your program?

_____

_____

_____

c. How can you apply the principle of <u>extinction</u> in a way that will raise the probability of your sticking to the program?

_____

_____

d. How can you use what you know about <u>shaping</u> to raise the probability that you will move efficiently through your program?

_____

_____

_____

e. How can you use what you know about <u>avoidance</u> to help yourself engage in your program as fully as possible?

_____

_____

Situation #2

Briefly describe another goal or subgoal you are trying to achieve and the principal elements of the program you have designed to achieve it.

_____

_____

_____

_____

a. How might you use reinforcement to strengthen your participation in the program? What incentives will work best for you?

_____

_____

_____

b. How might you use facilitative self-punishment to strengthen your participation in the program?

_____

_____

_____

c. How might you use extinction to strengthen your participation in the program?

_____

_____

_____

d. How might you use shaping to strengthen your participation in your program?

_____

_____

_____

e. How might you use what you know about avoidance to strengthen your participation in your program?

TASK 8: EVALUATING THE HELPING PROCESS

EXERCISE 63: Monitoring and evaluating current programs

One of the main reasons problem-management programs fail is that they are not monitored. Participation in a program slacks off sometimes without even being noticed. This means that monitoring has not been built into the program itself.

In this exercise you are asked to examine a program in which you are currently engaged and to ask yourself some monitoring questions. These questions are:

1. Are you participating or not?
     Client: "I checked with the doctor and set up a reasonable diet, but to tell the truth, I haven't started it yet. I've been more or less just trying to cut down on what I eat."
     Counselor: "With what kind of results?"
     Client: "I'm not sure. I haven't really checked."

2. If you are participating, how fully are you participating? What are you doing? What are you failing to do?
     Todd and Sue had agreed to talk out petty annoyances with each other instead of saving them up as a way of bettering their marriage. Sue said that she was doing this except when the annoyance included feelings of hurt. Todd said that he was doing this except when he felt his annoyance was too petty to discuss. Therefore, neither was participating fully in the program.

3. In what ways is monitoring built into the program itself?
     The staff at the rehabilitation center had weekly conferences with Roberta to discuss her progress in the physical therapy part of the rehabilitation program. She monitored her psychological progress through weekly meetings with a counselor. She reviewed with him the tasks she had set herself in the previous meeting. For instance, she discussed the times she allowed herself to engage in self-defeating self-talk.

4. Are there some clear indications that by participating in the program or subprogram you are moving toward your goal or subgoal? What are these indications?
     Sue and Todd discovered that the number of fights and arguments per week were actually diminishing. They also discovered that the fights they did have were not as bitter as they used to be. They were fighting more fairly with each other.

5. If the goal has been totally or even partially achieved, has it lead to or is it leading to some kind of effective management of the original problem situation?
     Jason's original presenting complaint was a "poor self image." This included feeling bad about his personal appearance. Since he was severely overweight, one goal was weight loss. He participated successfully in a weight loss program. When he lost a fair amount of weight, he began to feel better about himself in two ways. He felt 149

better about his physical appearance. And he now saw himself as an agent in life rather than a victim. He was on his way to handling his "poor self-image."

Now ask these same questions of a program in which you are presently engaged.

a. <u>A summary of your goal and program:</u>

_____

_____

_____

_____

_____

_____

b. Are you participating in the program or not?

_____

c. If you are participating, how fully are you participating? What are you doing? What are you failing to do?

_____

_____

_____

_____

What changes, if any, are needed in the program?

_____

_____

_____

_____

d. In what ways is monitoring built into the program itself?

_____

_____

_____

_____

How can you more effectively monitor your participation in the program?

_____

_____

_____

e. Are there some clear indications that by participating in this program or subprogram you are moving toward your goal or subgoal? What are these indications?

_____

_____

_____

_____

_____

What modifications, if any, do you have to make in your goals?

_____

_____

_____

f. If your goal has been fully or even partially accomplished, has it lead to or is it leading to some kind of effective management of the original problem situation or some part of it? How can you tell?

_____

_____

_____

_____

What kind of recycling of the helping process would be useful at this point?

_____

_____

_____

_____

EXERCISE 64: Positive learnings from programs that failed--a problem-management checklist

The philosopher Santayana suggested that those who don't learn from history are doomed to repeat it. Therefore, evaluating past programs that failed for one reason or another can be a most positive and useful exercise.

In this exercise you are asked to review a program that failed with a view to identifying the precise reasons for its failure. A checklist of the entire helping process will be used to do this.

Write a brief summary of a program that failed.

_____

_____

_____

_____

_____

_____

Now use the following checklist which involves the eight tasks of the helping process to examine possible sources of failure. You can use this checklist to ask yourself both what went right and what went wrong.

I. Problem definition and clarification

Task 1: Assessment.

* To what degree was your problem situation set in some kind of wider perspective, for instance, in terms of the relevant developmental events and the relevant social settings of your life?

_____

_____

_____

* To what degree was an attempt made to see to it that relevant resources, including personal and environmental, and values emerged during the exploration process?

_____

_____

_____

Task 2: Problem focusing and exploration

* To what degree did you focus one specific issue at a time or at least a small enough number to handle well?

_____

_____

_____

* To what degree were problems explored in terms of concrete, specific, and situation-related experiences, behaviors, and affect?

_____

_____

_____

* What indications are there that you spent either too much or too little time exploring the problem situation or some part of it from your perspective?

_____

_____

_____

Task 3: Developing new perspectives

* In what ways were you encouraged or did you encourage yourself to move beyond self-limiting views of your problem and develop new perspectives?

_____

_____

_____

* To what degree were these perspectives or "insights" related to setting problem-managing goals? That is, to what degree did these new perspectives or insights help you see the need for action?

_____

_____

_____

* To what degree did you achieve the kind of problem clarity that leads naturally to setting goals?

Task 4: Goal setting

* To what degree did you move beyond mere insights, declarations of intent, mission statements, and aims and set concrete and specific goals?

_____

_____

_____

* To what degree did whatever goals you set have the characteristics of workable goals, that is, to what degree were they stated as accomplishments, clear, measurable, realistic, adequate, in keeping with your values, and set in a reasonable time frame?

_____

_____

_____

Task 5: Exploration of program possibilities

* To what degree did you explore different ways of achieving your goals?

_____

_____

_____

* To what degree did you explore the consequences of different kinds of programs?

_____

_____

_____

Task 6: Choosing "best-fit" programs

* To what extent did you choose programs in keeping with your resources, values, and preferences?

_____

_____

_____

* To what extent did you identify <u>major steps (subgoals)</u> toward your goal and arrange for a workable progression toward each subgoal and the principal goal itself?

_____

_____

_____

Task 7: Implementation of programs

* To what extent did you foresee <u>critical obstacles</u> to the implementation of your program and prepare for them?

_____

_____

_____

* To what degree did you make sure that there were enough <u>incentives</u> for sticking to your program?

_____

_____

_____

* To what degree did you use other <u>principles of behavior</u> such as punishment, extinction, shaping, and avoidance to help you stick to your program?

_____

_____

_____

* To what degree did you find within yourself and in others sources of <u>support and challenge</u> to help you stick to your program?

_____

_____

_____

Task 8: Monitoring and evaluating the helping process

* To what degree was monitoring built into the helping process?

_____

_____

_____

* To what degree did you make modifications in any part of the helping process?

_____

_____

_____

* To what degree did you <u>recycle</u> the helping process or any part of it when what you were doing was not working out?

_____

_____

_____